RASPBERRY PI
FOR KIDS
MADE EASY

Raspberry Pi 3

element14
element14.com

Raspberry Pi 3
Model B

Wireless LAN

Bluetooth

Publisher and Creative Director: Nick Wells
Project Editors: Polly Prior and Laura Bulbeck
Art Director: Mike Spender
Layout Design: Jane Ashley
Digital Design and Production: Chris Herbert
Copy Editor: Katharine Davies
Technical Editor: Mark Mayne
Proofreader: Amanda Crook
Indexer: Eileen Cox
Special thanks to: Katherine Hawkins, Gillian Whitaker, Josie Mitchell, Frances Bodiam and Helen Crust.

FLAME TREE PUBLISHING
6 Melbray Mews
Fulham, London SW6 3NS
United Kingdom

www.flametreepublishing.com

First published 2015

15 17 19 18 16
1 3 5 7 9 10 8 6 4 2

A CIP record for this book is available from the British Library upon request.

ISBN: 978-1-78664-538-8

Printed in China | Created, Developed & Produced in the United Kingdom

Images are Courtesy of Shutterstock.com and the following: 3 alexmillos; 4(t), 14 Zoltan Kiraly; 4(b), 42 Dmytro Zinkevych; 5(t), 68 wavebreakmedia; 5(b), 106, Patrizio Martorana; 6(t), 142 JoemanjiArts; 6(b), 176 Piotr Adamowicz; 7(t), 212 ChristianChan; 7(b), 236 dizain; 8, 148 Syda Productions; 11(t) Victor Brave; 13 Dominik Zorgie; 16 Monkey Business Images; 18 Beresnev; 24(r) supot phanna; 27(b) Chikovnaya; 29(t) Nobelus; 37(b) Kekyalyaynen; 39(t) dedMazay; 39(b,r) notkoo; 41(t) Donna Apsey; 46(b) Voronin76; 48 Olivier Le Moal; 50 Vlasov Volodymyr; 82 Ollyy; 83(b) bbernard; 108, 171 Rawpixel.com; 109 Chepko Danil Vitalevich; 110 Ianych; 112(t) MaIII Themd; 113 Jan-Jacob Luijendijk; 116 Miroslav Hlavko; 117 Creativa Images; 118 Jaromir Chalabala; 120 AnnaIA; 122 Volodymyr Baleha; 123 Brian A Jackson; 124 Christi Tolbert; 125 efegraph; 127(t) Olesia Bilkei; 127(b) tanuha2001; 128(t) Tungphoto; 131 Sunny studio; 132(t) Svetislav1944; 132(b) racorn; 134 TonyV3112; 138 Tony Northrup; 139 Sumit buranaroththrakul; 144 Sergey Nivens; 146 maceira; 147 bestfoto77; 151 mirtmirt; 153(t) ronstik; 155 JuliusKielaitis; 157 Ijansempoi; 158 PR Image Factory; 159, 160 Iconic Bestiary; 161 Ironsv; 164 pio3; 168 Halfpoint; 169(b) Lerche&Johnson; 172(b) tanuha2001; 172(t) Nejron Photo; 174 Oez; 175 Ichumpitaz; 183 agsandrew; 187 frank_peters; 191 Lucky Business; 192 Ruslan Mitin; 194(b) woaiss; 197(t) kwanchai.c; 198 Yuganov Konstantin; 200 Ewais; 201 citybrabus; 203 anigoweb; 208 l l g h t p o e t; 218 Martina Vaculikova; 219(t) Designua; 222(b) ra3rn; 225(t) Albrus; 229(b) Mark Caunt; 233 Sergey Peterman; 234(b) Alexander Kazantsev; 241 Lipskiy; 247 alexytrener; 248 Catalin Petolea; 249 gcpics; 250 Aleksandr Veremeev; and Hot Tips courtesy of P and P Studio; Yayayoyo; Snezhana Togoi; Visual Generation; Dmitry Natashin; Irina Levitskaya; tani85fr; owatta; krasivo; Klara Viskova; NotionPic; Iconic Bestiary.

© Flickr and the following: 1, 21(t), 24(l), 26(b), 27(t), 111, 226, 227 Gareth Halfacree; 17(t) Nico Kaiser; 19 Open Knowledge Foundation Deutschland; 37(b) Fran Gil; 38 Clive Darra; 47(t) freeforcommercialuse.org/osde8info; 67(b) freeforcommercialuse.org/Riley Porter; 240 Christian Jann; 243 OxF2; 251 Neil Thompson.

© YouTube.com and the following: 49 Mark Bruce; 52 Dustin Kirkland.
instructables.com and the following: 59(b); 62(t), 145, 149, 150, 156, 231(b) Simon Monk; 63 Phillip Burgess; 173, 174, 175 koff1979.
Adafruit.com and the following: 64, 65, 66, 67(t), 230, 231(t), 234(t), 235, 244; 112(b) David Hunt; 169(t), 170 Spencer Organ; 173, 135, 136, 137 Ruiz Brothers; 202(b), 203 Tony DiCola.

Courtesy of Wikimedia Commons and the following: 79(t); 20 DanielJohnStevens; 27(t) Florian Frankenberger; 26(t) Jwrodgers; 28 Multicherry; 37(t) BengtLueers; 41(b) Luca Sbardella; 44 Ayaita; 45(t) D-Kuru; 45(b) Aidan C. Siegel; 46 Evan-Amos; 47 Asim18; 71(b) Magnus Manske; 154(t) Kmetamorphosis (GNU license); 238 Jared Smith.

Sam Pegg: 59(t), 60, 61, 62(b), 75, 76, 77, 81, 82, 83(t&c), 84, 85, 86, 87, 88, 89, 90, 92, 93, 94, 95, 96, 97, 98, 99, 103(b); © David Bryan: 119, 121; © Grant Gibson: 126, 128(b), 129; Chris Smith: 130, 153(b), 154(b), 178, 179, 180, 181, 182, 184, 185, 186(t), 188, 189, 190, 193, 194(t), 195, 197(b), 198(b), 202(t); Richard Hayler 215(b); spacemonkey.

Others: 9(t&b), 10, 11, 30, 31, 36, 47(c), 242, 246(t) RaspberryPi.org; 12 Tindie Inc; 17(b) School of Electronics and Computer Science, Southampton Uni, via Twitter user @ECSUoS; 29(b) UsualPanic.com; 32, 33(t&b), 34 © 2015 Kano Computing Ltd; 35 © Copyright 2015 FuzeBox I All rights reserved; 51(t), 54(b) Linuxlinks.com; 51(b), 73(b) © 2001-2015 Softpedia. All rights reserved; 53 lwn.net; 54(t) phuonguzi.wordpress.com; 55 (t&b) svrsig.org; 56(t) globlib4u.wordpress.com; 56(b) hreikin.wordpress.com; 57 HTPCbeginner.com; 70 micromart.co.uk/David Briddock; 71(t) quick2wire.com; 72 TechTarget/Yasir Irfan; 73(t) cdathenry.wordpress.com; 74 Pixabay/mojzagrebinfo; 78 RasPi.TV; 79(b) Stackoverflow.com; 80(t) Windows 8 Downloads http://bit.ly/1PeSFF3; 80(b) Malin Christensson, Malinc http://bit.ly/11C22tY; 91 Tjhsst.edu; 100 Bloodshed.net; 102(b) blog.idrsolutions.com; 102(t) Codecall.net; 103(t) Planetgeek.ch; 104(b) forum.osdev.org; 104(t) Davidbriddock.blogspot.co.uk; 114, 115 © Naturebytes.org; 140, 141 © PiBorg.org; 163, 165, 166, 167 Copyright 2015 © EDIMAX Technology Co., Ltd. All Rights Reserved; 186(b) © 2015 HiFiBerry; 196, 199 facebook.com/motionpie; 204, 205, 206, 207 osmc.tv; 209, 211 Raspberry-Spy.co.uk; 210(b) © 2015 RAVPower Inc. All rights reserved; 214, 215(t&c), 220, 221, 228, 229(t), 232 Amazon.co.uk - via PR; 216, 217 pythonprogramming.net; 222(t); 223, 224, 225(b) www.pocketmoneytronics.co.uk; 239 2015 Broadcom Corporation; 245 Pidome.wordpress.com; 246(b) Artem.gratchev.com.

RASPBERRY PI
FOR KIDS
MADE EASY

MARK MAYNE, SAMUEL HORTI,
RENE MILLMAN, CHRIS SMITH
& LAURENCE MOZAFARI

FLAME TREE
PUBLISHING

CONTENTS

For those new to the Raspberry Pi, this chapter will introduce you to the model itself as well as provide an overview of its best features. Here you'll have the opportunity to learn all about the foundations of the model, explore the device iterations in more detail and take a look at some of the kits that are currently available for the Raspberry Pi. We'll also discuss everything you will need to know about the optional hardware, such as how to use the camera and audio settings, and also provide hot tips throughout on how to get the most out of your Pi.

This chapter will walk you through the process of getting started with your Raspberry Pi. From choosing an OS to learning your way around the booting process, this chapter will help guide you through all of the early stages.

In order to get your Raspberry Pi up and running you will need to know about programming. In this chapter, you will learn really useful information about the basics of programming as well as the different options available to you. We'll also explain the differences between programming in Scratch and in Python in more detail.

There are so many things that can be done with the Raspberry Pi and this chapter introduces you to just a few of the exciting projects and gadgets available. From building your own mobile phone to creating an automated pet feeder, here you will find lots of creative ways to have fun while using your Raspberry Pi.

RASPBERRY PI & THE INTERNET............142

If you are looking to set the internet up on your Raspberry Pi, this chapter will offer you all the necessary advice and help to do so. You'll learn how to make a Wi-Fi router and hotspot, build your own internet radio, and also find information on how to create your very own personal cloud server.

RASPBERRY PI & AUDIO & VIDEO...........176

For those of you who are looking to be really creative with your Raspberry Pi, this chapter will offer you great ideas on how to do so. We'll offer tips on how to successfully stream videos, supply straightforward guides on how to make your very own video capture unit and also explore exciting network streaming projects that you can get to grips with.

As you become more confident with
your Raspberry Pi, you may want to go
a little further and explore more ways
in which your Pi can be used. Here, you
will find a range of ideas on how to
keep your Pi in tiptop condition, such
as making or buying a case. We'll also
discuss the ins and outs of overclocking
as well as provide you with more
unusual project ideas to keep you busy.

There may be times where you run into trouble
with your Raspberry Pi, but fear not – this final
chapter will provide you with useful technical
support. This chapter covers the most common
problems that occur with the Raspberry Pi and
offers the best solutions. From helping you
to test your power supply, tackling any Wi-Fi
issues you may have and also providing you
with troubleshooting tips, this chapter tells you
everything you need to know.

INTRODUCTION

The Raspberry Pi is a tiny bundle of mini PC joy that has kept millions amused and in the process has built thousands of awesome creations. Far more than the sum of its parts, the original low-cost, programmable PC platform has taken the computing community by storm.

From dedicated hobbyists of all ages, to parents, teachers and schools encouraging children and students to understand and engage with technology, through to a tool for impoverished nations to get their economies going, the Raspberry Pi is the platform of choice.

Now you can join in the fun as well, with this easy-to-follow guide and just a few pounds' worth of standard computer hardware. We'll guide you every step of the way, from the initial choices of essential gear, through setting up your ideal configuration to the exciting bit – amazing projects that'll inspire you and actually come in handy, too.

In the process you'll learn about how technology works, and can explore as far as your fancy takes you into the world of computing, which increasingly powers much of our daily lives.

EVERYTHING YOU NEED TO KNOW

The Raspberry Pi was originally conceived back in 2006, and after many prototypes became a commercial reality in 2012. It was intended to be a low-cost entry-level PC that would help a new generation get into programming. The founders, Eben Upton, Rob Mullins, Jack Lang and Alan Mycroft, based at the University of Cambridge's Computer Laboratory, felt that the explosion in prohibitively complex technology, such as games consoles and smartphones, was preventing young people from engaging with the creative side of technology, such as writing software and building hardware projects.

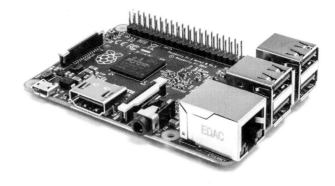

Above: Raspberry Pi B circuit board side view.

The founders decided: 'Something had changed the way kids were interacting with computers. A number of problems were identified: the colonization of the ICT curriculum with lessons on using Word and Excel, or writing webpages; the end of the dot-com boom; and the rise of the home PC and games console to replace the Amigas, BBC Micros, Spectrum ZX and Commodore 64 machines that people of an earlier generation learned to program on.'

Thus the Raspberry Pi 1 Model A was born, the first in a series of incrementally-improved but simple mini PCs.

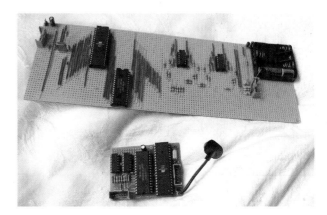

Above: An early Raspberry Pi prototype.

The idea caught on extraordinarily rapidly, and an ardent community germinated, expanded daily and took an active role in determining how the platform developed. The result is one of the most vibrant computing communities on the planet, which has collectively created countless replicable projects for every taste. Whether you're looking to build a specific item, such as a robot, smartphone or camera, or something even more obscure and ingenious, the Raspberry Pi will come in a flavour to suit.

This book seeks to help and inspire, no matter how deep you want to go, and will also be a handy reference guide in the rare event of projects not going to plan and you needing troubleshooting aid.

BITE-SIZE INFORMATION

As a practical guide to the Raspberry Pi, you don't need to read this book from cover to cover. It is organized so that you can dip into the different areas that are relevant to you, as and when needed, whether that's setting up, troubleshooting or getting inspired with great new projects.

Each section stands alone and includes simple guides to building the projects described, or at least a similar version, customized to your own tastes. For example, in one section you learn how to add peripherals to your basic set-up, while in another you discover how to choose an OS, which could culminate in you building a working robot.

Above: Raspberry Pi Zero circuit board.

STEP BY STEP

Throughout the book, step-by-step guides take you through each stage of a project or advanced set-up, showing you exactly what to do. Each section gives clear, concise instructions about what needs to be done, as well as hot tips to make the projects and tasks easier.

HELP!

In the unlikely event you do get really stuck on a particular topic, we're here to help. Simply email your query to Flame Tree Publishing at support@ flametreepublishing.com. While we cannot operate a 24-hour helpline to cover the complete range of Raspberry Pi problems, we will respond by email as soon as possible.

YOUR GUIDE

If you have never played around with the Raspberry Pi before, this book will soon get you up and running. There's also plenty for the more experienced user to discover, with more advanced information as well. Our expert authors will introduce you to a broad range of projects, set-ups and ideas to get your creative juices flowing, and you'll soon be developing your own.

Above: Raspberry Pi Model B circuit board.

Above: Raspberry Pi camera accessory.

FROM BEGINNER TO EXPERT

This book will take you through the essentials of the Raspberry Pi over the course of eight chapters, starting with how to set up a Raspberry Pi and the additional items you need, and then guiding you through the software options. Each chapter has a series of inspiring projects to take on, which gradually become more advanced as your skill and confidence build. Finally, there's information about linking up the Raspberry Pi to other peripherals and systems to create even more exciting projects.

DIFFERENT MODELS

If you're a newcomer to the Raspberry Pi we expect you'll likely be using one of the most recent models, the Pi 3 or Pi Zero. There are a wide range of different models of the Pi you can choose from, and you should note that the authors have used a range of models throughout this book. Chapter 1 will guide you through the different versions and any major differences.

EIGHT CHAPTERS

After taking you through the set-up options in Chapters 1 and 2, it's time to start on your programming skills. We begin with Scratch, a more visual, building block-based programming method, before striking out into Python. We'll touch on other languages that are commonly used, too – the only limit is your imagination.

Chapter 4 brings you some stunning ideas to take you even deeper into the world of the Raspberry Pi, such as real robots, incredible toys and even building your own smartphone. There's the world's smallest Mac to build, too, or if you keep your own hens, there's a chicken coop minder that's quite simply genius. Then Chapter 5 sees us go online, create networking projects that'll improve any home, as well as touch on media storage and streaming.

Chapter 6 digs deeper into the world of home entertainment, with tips on building your own media centre and even a spycam. Chapter 7 takes this further, showing you how to literally build on your Pi platform with Arduino and external components, via breadboarding and soldering, as well as a flavour of some of the almost infinite options for creating a case for your Pi.

Hot Tips

All through the book, Hot Tips provide quick and handy information about how to get more from your Raspberry Pi. They also highlight the best techniques to help you to become an expert user.

Finally, Chapter 8 deals with common troubleshooting techniques and top tips to get out of trouble fast.

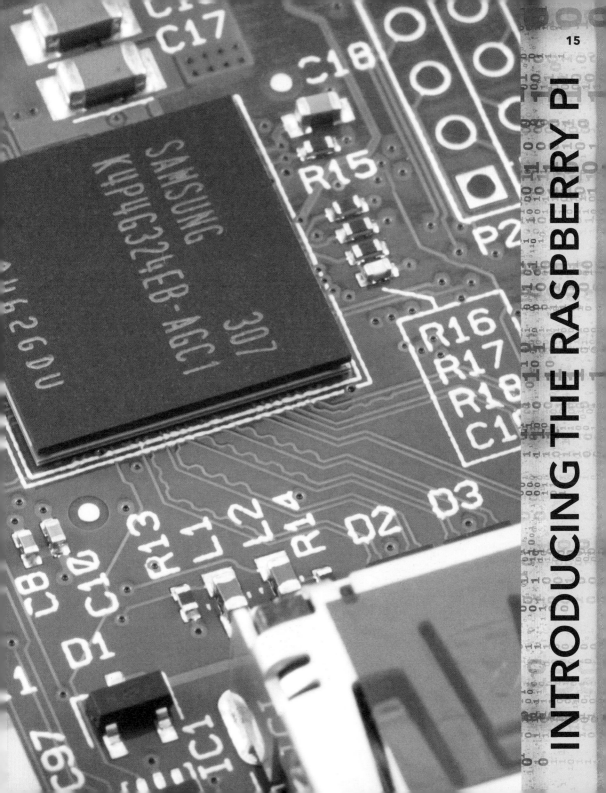

INTRODUCING THE RASPBERRY PI

WHAT IS THE RASPBERRY PI?

The Raspberry Pi is a credit card-sized computer that plugs directly into a monitor or your home TV, and uses a standard PC keyboard and mouse. It was dreamt up as a device for teaching children computer science, and since its release in 2012, it has been helping young and old alike to program via a number of easy-to-use applications.

It can be bought at a range of low-pricepoints and is designed to be easy to set up and use. You buy a Pi, plug in the peripherals, download a Linux operating system, and away you go.

But it's also a versatile device that does everything you'd expect a computer to do – it can browse the internet, stream high-definition video, play games and create spreadsheets. From powering robot rhinos to running an HD home surveillance camera, the Pi proves that you don't need to splash the cash to build an advanced computer system.

Above: The Raspberry Pi is cheap and versatile – what more could you want?

COOL PI PROJECTS

Since the Pi first arrived, people all over the world have used it to power countless projects – and you could be doing the same very soon.

Erica the Rhino

It doesn't get much cooler than a robot rhino. The Electronics and Computer Science department at the University of Southampton has created Erica, a rhino powered by five Raspberry Pis. Erica can growl like a real rhino, move her ears, read and send out tweets, and interact with people nearby via their smartphones.

The Picrowave

No, it's not a pie-warming device, it's something far better: a Raspberry Pi-powered microwave. Nathan Broadbent decided his Pi would best serve his stomach, so he incorporated it into his kitchen by taking his own food-zapper apart. It goes further than a traditional microwave, too – the Picrowave can scan food barcodes to look up cooking times, tweet when the food is cooked, and recognize your voice. Tasty stuff.

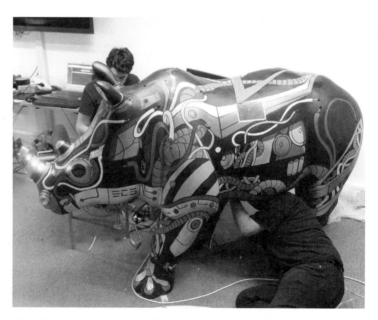

Above: Erica is a robotic rhino powered by Pi.

THE PI FOUNDATION

The Raspberry Pi Foundation is a registered educational charity based in the UK. Its goal is to promote the education of children in the field of computers and computer science. Through its education fund, it helps pay for schemes around the globe, and has completed projects from Afghanistan to Cambridge.

HOW IT ALL BEGAN

Twenty years ago, young people needed to code computers in order to use them – nowadays, kids can use powerful devices without knowing how they work.

In 2006, staff at the University of Cambridge Computer Laboratory became concerned about the decline in both the number and skills of applicants to the university's computer science courses.

Hot Tip

David Braben, co-author of the seminal BBC Micro game Elite, is one of the Foundation's co-founders.

They gave birth to the idea of the Raspberry Pi – a cheap, easy-to-program computer that would help children get to grips with programming. After six years of work, their dream became a reality when the first Raspberry Pi launched in 2012.

RASPBERRY JAMS

Arguably one of the Foundation's biggest achievements – as if the gift of programming and encouraging worldwide charity is not enough – is cultivating an engaged community of Pi enthusiasts, eager to learn from each other.

This enthusiasm manifests itself in the wonderfully named Raspberry Jams. These are events organized all over the world, where Pi lovers gather to share knowledge, show off their newest Pi-based contraptions and generally spread the word about what Pi can offer.

There's a wealth of community support you can get without attending these events, too, such as magazines, newsletters, blogs, YouTube channels and much more.

Above: The Foundation's focus is computer education for children.

ITERATIONS OF THE DEVICE

There are actually a few versions of the Raspberry Pi – which we'll examine in more detail later in the chapter – but first, let's talk about what they have in common: the Pi's building blocks, if you like.

○ **System on a chip**: The Pi is built around a system on a chip (SoC) – a method of putting everything you need to run a computer on to a single chip. This eliminates the need for separate chips for computing (CPUs), graphics (GPUs), memory (RAM) and USB controllers.

Hot Tip

The first SoC was used in 1970, in the Hamilton Pulsar Wrist Computer.

○ **SD card**: Every computer needs an operating system, and the Pi's – Linux – sits on an SD card, which plugs into the circuit board.

Above: The Pi's operating system is stored on an SD card.

○ **USB ports**: The Pi doesn't do much just sitting by itself. You need to hook it up to other devices – keyboard, mouse and so on – through the USB or micro USB port, so you can actually do something useful.

- **GPIOs**: General purpose input/output connections enable you to connect the Pi to the outside world. As their name suggests, they can receive inputs and give outputs in a variety of ways, such as sensors and LEDs.

- **Audio and video**: Many Pi programs rely on pictures and sound. Pis have video outputs for TVs and monitors – HDMI or component – as well as audio outputs that enable you to hook them up to speakers or headphones.

Above: GPIOs connect the Pi to the outside world.

- **Internet**: As you'd expect in today's connected world, most models of the Pi can connect to the internet via a built-in Ethernet cable, although newer models connect over Wi-Fi.

The Three Flavours of Pi

- **Model A/B**: A newer version of the original Model A, the A+ was a lower spec version of the Pi A. Then came models B and B+, which improved computing power considerably.

- **Model 2B**: The second generation of Raspberry Pi – the Pi 2 – added significantly more power and was the standard reference model until...

- **Model 3B**: The latest version of a full-fat Raspberry Pi packs a real punch, with a Quad-Core 64bit CPU, as well as WiFi & Bluetooth.

- **Model Zero/Zero W**: The newest Pi models, the Zero and Zero W are much smaller than their siblings, but still deliver great specs at a super-low cost. The Zero W layers on WiFi & Bluetooth connections.

BASIC DESIGN

The boards of the Pis vary greatly from one another – we'll delve into the details in just a moment. On this page you can see a diagram of the Raspberry Pi 3 Model B, the latest version of the device. Here's an explanation of how it all fits together (*see* pages 26–31 for more on the hardware and components described below).

BOARD DIAGRAM

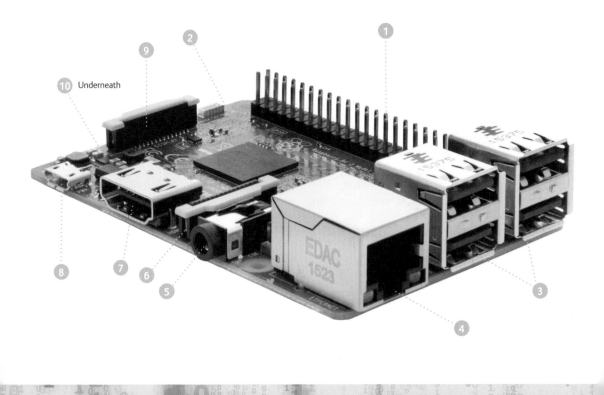

Hot Tip

Schematics of all models of the Pi are available through the official website.

1 GPIO pins: The pins sit along one edge of the board, giving easy access to input and output connections.

2 SoC: The Broadcom DCM2830 family of SoCs sits at the centre of all the Pis, housing the computer processing unit (CPU), the graphical processing unit (GPU), memory (RAM) and a digital signal processor, which measures, filters and compresses analogue signals.

3 USB ports: Their number varies from one to four, depending on your choice of Pi. Use them to connect your Pi to peripherals, such as a keyboard, mouse, external storage (hard drive) or a wireless dongle.

4 Ethernet port: Present on most Pis, this port connects the Pi to the internet or a network. The Pi 3B and Zero W have onboard Wi-Fi, other devices will need an adaptor.

5 Audio jack/composite video: A new addition for the Model B+, this socket eliminates the need for a separate composite video socket. The socket carries both audio and video signals. Cables that match it are widely available.

6 CSI camera connector: Get snappy with your Pi by using the device's camera, which is sold separately.

7 HDMI port: The Pi works with almost any monitor or TV, and an HDMI connection is the simplest way of connecting it to modern displays.

8 Power supply: You supply power to the Pi through a 5 V micro USB charger, similar to the ones used by smartphones.

9 DSI display connector: Own an LCD TV? No problem for the Pi – wire it up here using a 15-pin ribbon cable.

10 SD card slot: Your micro SD card fits neatly on to the Pi's underbelly.

PI 1: FIRST GENERATION

The Pi 1 is the term for the first generation of Pi devices, of which there are several. Originally released as the Model A – a low-cost variant of the Pi – and the Model B, the boards have now been upgraded and sold as the Model A+ and Model B+. They have since been superseded by the Pi 2, Pi 3 and Pi Zeros, but are still available.

Above: The Model A.

Model A Specs

- **SoC:** Broadcom BCM2835.

- **CPU:** 700 MHz single-core ARM1176JZF-S.

- **GPU:** Broadcom VideoCore IV running at 250 MHz.

- **USB:** One USB port, direct from the SoC.

- **Memory:** 256 MB of synchronous dynamic random access memory (SDRAM), shared with the GPU.

- **Video input:** 15-pin camera interface (CSI) connector that works with the Raspberry Pi camera.

- **Video outputs:** HDMI supporting 14 different resolutions, from 640 x 350 up to 1,920 x 1,200; composite video output via an RCA connector.

- **Audio:** Analogue output via a 3.5 mm audio jack and digital via HDMI; output and input also occur via Integrated Interchip Sound.

Above: You can connect your Raspberry Pi to a monitor with an HDMI cable.

Hot Tip

Add a Wi-Fi dongle to your Model A for a great media centre to sit behind your TV.

- **Internet**: No Ethernet capability.

- **Power ratings**: 300 mA (1.5 V).

- **Power source**: 5 V via micro USB.

- **GPIO**: 26 GPIO connectors.

- **Storage**: SD card slot.

From A to A+: Key Differences

The Model A+ replaced the original Model A in November 2014. The key differences between the two products are outlined below.

Above: The Pi Model A+ added more ports to the low-cost Model A.

- **More control**: The number of General Purpose Input/Output (GPIO) pins – generic pins the behaviour of which the user can control – increased from 26 to 40.

- **Better micro SD slot**: The old friction-based SD socket of the Model A was replaced with a push-push socket in the A+, making the cards easier to use. The device also switched from SD to micro SD cards.

- **Lower power consumption**: By changing the device's power regulators, power usage was reduced by between 0.5 and 1W.

- **Better audio**: The Model A+ added a dedicated, low noise power supply for its audio circuit.

- **Slimmer, sleeker look**: By moving components around – which included aligning the USB connector with the board edge – the A+ is 2 cm shorter than its older brother. It's also a lot lighter – 23 g compared to 45 g.

THE MODEL B

The Model B – now the Model B+ – was the more powerful of the two first-generation Pi computers, enabling it to be used in more complex projects.

Above: The Model B is the original Pi – reliable, if outdated.

The Specs

- **SoC:** Broadcom BCM2835.

- **CPU:** 700 MHz single core ARM1176JZF-S.

- **GPU:** Broadcom VideoCore IV running at 250 MHz.

- **USB:** Two USB connections.

- **Memory:** 512 MB of SDRAM, shared with the GPU.

- **Video input:** 15-pin camera interface (CSI) connector that works with the Raspberry Pi camera.

- **Video outputs:** HDMI supporting 14 different resolutions; analogue video via 3.5 mm jack.

- **Audio:** Analogue output via a 3.5 mm audio jack and digital via HDMI.

- **Internet:** 10/100 Mbit/s Ethernet USB adapter.

- **Power ratings:** 700 mA (3.5 V).

- **Power source:** 5 V via micro USB.

- **GPIO:** 26 GPIO pins.

- **Storage:** SD card slot.

Above: A toy incorporating the Model B.

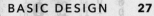

Above: The Pi Model B+.

From B to B+: Key Differences

- **Four USB slots:** A huge change that enables users to connect a keyboard, mouse and Wi-Fi dongle at the same time.

- **More GPIO pins:** The B+ boasts a whopping 40 GPIO pins, making it a much more versatile device.

- **Micro SD:** To replace the B's SD card.

Hot Tip

The B+ may represent an upgrade, but it actually costs about £6 ($10) less than the original B.

- **Lower power consumption:** By changing the device's power regulators, power usage was reduced by between 0.5 and 1W.

- **Better audio:** Dedicated, low noise power supply for its audio circuit.

- **Combined audio/video:** Analogue video is handled through a combined 3.5 mm jack, eliminating the need for a composite video port.

THE PI 2: A NEW BEAST

Released in early 2015, the Pi 2 Model B was more powerful, so it could run a full range of Linux distributions, as well as Microsoft Windows 10.

Tech Specs

- **SoC**: Broadcom BCM2836.

- **CPU**: 900 MHz quad-core ARM Cortex-A7.

- **GPU**: Broadcom VideoCore IV running at 250 MHz.

- **USB**: Four ports.

- **Memory**: 1 GB of SDRAM, shared with the GPU.

- **Video input**: 15-pin camera interface (CSI) connector that works with the Raspberry Pi camera.

- **Video outputs**: HDMI supporting 14 different resolutions; MIPI display interface for LCD displays.

- **Audio**: Analogue output via a 3.5 mm audio jack and digital via HDMI; output and input also occur via Integrated Interchip Sound.

Above: The second generation of Pi came with a raft of improvements.

THE RASPBERRY PI 3B

The Raspberry Pi 3B is the third generation Raspberry Pi, and launched in February 2016, replacing the Raspberry Pi 2 Model B as top dog. Luckily the Pi Foundation have kept precisely the same physical layout, so earlier cases, projects etc should still work fine.

Tech Specs

○ **Powerful:** The Pi 3B is more powerful again than its older siblings, now boasting a Broadcom BCM2387 chipset with a 1.2GHz 64-bit quad-core ARMv8 CPU, capable of running pretty much anything: Windows 10, Linux, it's all your jam.

○ **Wireless:** The new Broadcom package includes baked in 802.11n Wireless LAN (no more adaptors!), as well as Bluetooth 4.1 and Bluetooth Low Energy (BLE). It's a flexible, fully wireless package.

○ **Power requirements:** These are slightly up on the Pi 2, at 2.5A, although RAM is the same, at 1GB.

You'll recognize the specs below as they are the same as on the Pi 2 B. This is deliberate so all project schematics still make sense!

Like the Pi 2, it also has: 4 USB ports, 40 GPIO pins, full HDMI port, ethernet port, combined 3.5mm audio jack and composite video, camera interface (CSI), display interface (DSI), micro SD card slot (now push-pull rather than push-push) and a VideoCore IV 3D graphics score.

Above: Choose your Pi and begin building your projects.

Above: Raspberry Pi Zero with camera connector.

RASPBERRY PI ZERO AND ZERO W

In November 2015 the Pi Foundation surprised everyone with a new model that offered a range of upgrades and a lower price. The Raspberry Pi Zero was unleashed, and the following year in February 2017 the Foundation released the most recent variant of the Zero, the Zero W, which builds on the spec of the Zero with wireless LAN and Bluetooth priced at only £9.60 ($10).

Pi Zero Specs

- **Processor:** Broadcom BCM2835 application processor with a 1GHz ARM11 core.

- **RAM:** 512 MB of LPDDR2 SD.

- **Storage:** Micro-SD card slot.

- **Video output:** Mini-HDMI socket for 1080p60.

- **Data and power:** Micro-USB sockets.

- **GPIO:** An unpopulated 40-pin GPIO header, rather brilliantly with the same pinout as Pi Model A+/B+/2B versions, so projects will transfer across seamlessly.

- **Video:** An unpopulated composite video header.

- **Power:** A power requirement of 1.2 A.

○ **Form**: The smallest ever, at an almost microscopic 65 mm x 30 mm x 5 mm.

Raspberry Pi Zero W

The Raspberry Pi Zero W has all the functionality of the original Pi Zero but with added connectivity, consisting of: 802.11 b/g/n wireless LAN; Bluetooth 4.1 and Bluetooth Low Energy (BLE).

Above: The Raspberry Pi Zero W.

WHAT'S ALL THE FUSS ABOUT?

The boost in power in the Pi 3B is a huge deal, and its wireless smarts really add up to a complete package. Not only is it the most powerful Pi so far but the price has barely increased at all as it costs around £32 ($41).

WHICH MODEL SHOULD I USE?

The Foundation recommends using different Pi models for different needs.

○ **Pi 3B**: The Pi 3B is the new king of the hill, and will be the model you'll find in school labs and homes alike - the natural successor to the Model 2B. The 2B is still available, but the cost saving versus computing power isn't significant.

○ **Pi Zero**: The latest model, the Pi Zero is recommended for embedded or low-power projects, as is the much older, but still handy Model A+.

○ **Wi-Fi and Bluetooth**: The Pi 3B and Pi Zero W both have on-board Wi-Fi and Bluetooth, so if you're planning a wireless build then these two should be top of your list.

RASPBERRY PI KITS

You can buy the Raspberry Pi directly from the Foundation and associated suppliers, but you only get the Pi itself. To a complete beginner, the idea of starting with nothing but a circuit board can be quite daunting.

To make it easier, companies have started bundling Pis with other products and selling them as kits, which you can buy for a higher price.

Hot Tip

Kano ships free to most countries across the world.

WHAT ARE RASPBERRY PI KITS?

Pi kits are computer kits based on the Pi, which contain the Pi and various extras, depending on which one you plump for. They range from kits that contain their own operating system and manual – such as the Kano kit, which we'll look at in more detail in a moment – to simple bundles containing the Pi and a set of peripherals, such as a case, power leads and more.

Above: Pi kits give you everything you need to start using your Pi.

KANO KIT

The £139.99 ($180) Kano is one of the most popular Raspberry Pi kits on the market. Funded via a $1.5 million Kickstarter campaign – backed by high-profile tech figures including Apple co-founder Steve Wozniak – it aims to simplify the process of starting out with the Pi.

Above: The Kano Kit is one of the most popular kits around.

What's in the Box?

- **Raspberry Pi 3B**: Kano uses the latest Pi for maximum flexibility.

- **Instructional books**: 'Manuals are boring,' Kano says. These books are stories in which you can make up your own characters and level while following clear, illustrated steps to build your computer.

- **DIY speaker**: Built to hook up to the Pi, the speaker gives you the first chance to test your building prowess.

- **Keyboard**: And a very stylish one at that. It's small enough to hold like a game controller, wireless, has an integrated touchpad and independent click buttons. What's not to like?

- **Kano OS**: Kano has created its own operating system to make learning programming even easier. It's open source, sleek and a great starter tool.

Above: The Kano OS is bright and colourful – perfect for kids.

◦ **SD card**: Your card comes pre-loaded with the Kano OS. It's an 8GB – for plenty of storage – Class 10 micro SD card, and comes with an SD adapter.

◦ **Pi case**: Kano has eschewed the more garish lids on the market and plumped for a clip-on transparent case, which you can customize by using case cards or by printing your own covers.

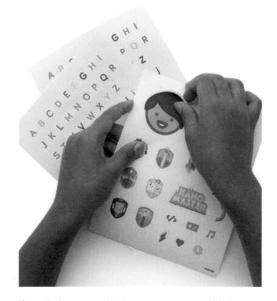

◦ **Stickers**: You're never too old for stickers; these are great for both kids and adults who never grew up.

Above: Stickers are possibly the most important part of the Kano Kit.

◦ **Cables**: There's no need to buy your own cables – Kano comes with an HDMI cable and a mini USB power plug.

◦ **DIY**: Kano's original kits were so popular that they now do a bumper 'make your own PC' version including an HD screen for just £264.99 ($342).

THE BEST OF THE REST

Kano is not the only kit on the market – here are some of the other big players.

Fuze T2-R

This is one of the more expensive kits around. It comes with the Pi 2B, a keyboard, USB hub – all the standard fare – as well as an electronics components kit featuring LEDs, switches and light sensors. Everything a budding builder needs.

Most excitingly, it comes with a robotic arm –
yes, you read that right – that you can assemble
yourself. Instructions are included, alongside
a general programming guide and solder-less
breadboard to enable you to experiment with
your circuitry.

Hot Tip

The cost of Pi kits can really
vary, so shop around before
choosing one.

Raspberry Pi 3 Retro Gaming Bundle

The Pi Hut's gaming bundle is relatively cheap at £65 ($84), but with a complete Pi 3B kit and
two 'SNES'-style controllers you'll be experiencing those retro gaming thrills in no time at all!

Pimoroni Starter Kit

A cheap and cheerful kit to get you up and running. It comes with a Pibow case in a range of
bright colours, along with a keyboard, mouse, power supply and stickers for you to plaster the
wall with. All the cables and plugs you need are also included; you just need your own display.

Above: Robot arm + Raspberry Pi = awesome fun.

REQUIRED HARDWARE

You've bought your Raspberry Pi, so what's next? You need a few more pieces of kit to get started.

SD CARD

Hot Tip

SD cards with NOOBS pre-installed can be found cheaply at the Foundation's Swag Store.

- **How big should it be?** The minimum recommended size is 8 GB. The Pi team recommends an 8 GB Class 4 SD card, so that's your best bet.

- **What's the maximum?** The Pi team says they have tried cards all the way up to 32 GB, and most work OK. If you want extra storage, you can attach a USB stick or – if you really need the space – a USB hard drive.

Above: NOOBS enables you to easily install your OS of choice.

- **NOOBS or not?** To use your Pi you need an operating system, and the easiest way to get one is using NOOBS, or New Out of the Box Software. You can buy an SD card with NOOBS pre-installed, or download it on to your existing card.

- **An SD card could save the device:** If you brick the device, you can always reflash the SD card.

Above: If you need a lot of storage space you can connect a USB hard drive.

DISPLAY

○ **What display can I use?** The Pi 3 features both an HDMI output and a 3.5 mm audio-video output, which means you can hook it up to a DVI/HDMI monitor or TV. Use a passive HDMI-to-DVI cable for DVI displays, or simply use an HDMI lead for HDMI displays. The HDMI output also supports Consumer Electronic Control (CEC), allowing your Pi to communicate back and forth with the display.

○ **What about older televisions?** For the Model A+, hook up your analogue TV using the composite lead or a composite-to-SCART connector. On the Model B+ and Pi 2B, the composite output has been replaced with a 3.5 mm combined audio and video output. To connect to older TVs, you need a 3.5 mm-to-3RCA adapter cable. Use one that's compatible with iPod video.

Above: The Pi connects straight to HDMI TVs and monitors.

○ **What about VGA support?** There's no direct VGA support on the Pi, and passive adapters don't work, so use an active HDMI-to-VGA converter that has its own power supply.

Above: Use an adapter to connect your DVI monitor to your Pi.

CONNECTIVITY CABLES

As well as your connection to your monitor, you need a standard Ethernet cable for internet access, unless you're planning to use Wi-Fi.

Hot Tip

Faulty power supplies can cause a lot of problems with the Pi. See 'Troubleshooting Power Problems' on pages 250–51.

KEYBOARD AND MOUSE

Any standard USB keyboard and mouse will do. The Model A/A+ has one USB port, the Model B has two ports and the the Model 2 and Model 3 versions have four ports each. Use a USB hub to connect more devices.

POWER SUPPLY

○ **Which power supply should I use?** Although most smartphone micro-USB chargers will work to some degree, the best option for the Pi 3B is the Official Raspberry Pi 5.1V 2.5A International Power Supply, which will take care of most project requirements and your PI to boot!

○ **Connecting high-powered devices to the Pi**: If you plan on using high-powered or high-current devices with the Pi – such as a USB hard drive – connect a powered USB hub, and plug the devices into this instead of directly into the Pi.

Above: A Pi with a USB hub.

OPTIONAL HARDWARE

If you want to do a little bit more with your Pi, here are some extra items you might find useful.

AUDIO

- **How can I listen to sound?** Connect headphones or earphones with a 3.5 mm jack to the Pi for audio.

- **Can I use a microphone?**
  Yes – make sure it's a USB microphone.

INTERNET CONNECTION

- **Ethernet cable:** Although the Pi 3 has built-in Wi-Fi, having an Ethernet cable can be handy for downloading big files or testing connections. Older models will need an Ethernet cable to connect to the internet to download or update software.

- **USB Wi-Fi dongle:** The Pi 3 and Pi Zero W both have onboard Wi-Fi, but all the other models will need a Wi-Fi dongle. The Pi Foundation sells a fully tested, branded dongle through its store.

CAMERA
Camera Board

The Pi camera board is a separate printed circuit board (PCB) that connects to the Pi. With a 15 cm ribbon cord, it plugs into the Pi's CSI-2 camera port, enabling you to use a camera module to snap still shots and videos. All models of the Pi can use the camera board.

Above: The Pi camera attaches to the Pi with a ribbon cord.

The Camera Itself

The camera module is Omnivision 5647, and is comparable to mobile phone cameras. It has a 5-megapixel lens, supporting 1080p video at 30 frames per second, 720p video at 60 frames per second and VGA90 video. It is the only camera compatible with the Pi, and it uses 250 mA of power.

Picture Formats

The camera can capture raw images, as well as JPEG, PNG, GIF and BMP, uncompressed YUV or uncompressed RGB. It records video in H.264, baseline, main or high-profile formats.

Power Requirements

The camera requires 250 mA – take this into account when deciding whether your power supply can power your Pi and all its peripherals.

Above: The Pi camera board can be used with all models of the Pi.

How Do I Use the Camera?

You use the camera through separate applications for video and stills. These apps have features comparable to those of compact cameras – you can set the size of the image, light sensitivity, image compression quality and exposure mode.

Camera Case Study: Your Own CCTV

You can turn your Pi into a high-definition surveillance camera. Enthusiast Christoph Buenger did just that by putting his Pi and camera board inside a fake CCTV camera case. It features motion detection, so if something moves in front of the camera, it records for a set period of time.

The files save directly to a shared Windows folder, and can stream footage online. Christoph can receive notifications when the camera detects motion, and could even incorporate a temperature sensor, if he felt so inclined.

Using the Camera: Bird Feeder Twitter

San Francisco-based Manifold has created a bird table that – using the Pi camera – snaps and tweets a picture of any bird that comes to it hungry for grub. An infrared sensor detects a landing bird and triggers the camera, with the photos automatically uploaded to Twitter. Look it up – @feedertweeter.

A CASE FOR YOUR PI

The Pi does not come with a case, but the protection a case offers your hardware makes it one of the more popular optional extras.

The Official Case

The Foundation offers its own case for the Pi, which costs just £6 ($10). It's sleek, leaves all the ports easily accessible, and its side plate can be removed so you can access the device's GPIO pins.

However, it's not the only case. There are lots of suppliers of cases, or you can make your own. Watch out for cheap fakes though, the real ones are better quality and contribute to the Pi Foundation charity as well!

Altoids Tin Case

It doesn't get more DIY than this. One Pi user discovered that the device fits inside a tin of Altoids breath mints. With a bit of drilling, and some patience, you can turn the tin into a perfectly serviceable case for your Pi. Find instructions on the Pi website.

Above: You can even build a case out of Lego.

GETTING STARTED

SETTING EVERYTHING UP

The Raspberry Pi is a great little computer for tinkering around with, but like a normal computer, it only works if you provide it with power and some way of inputting and outputting data.

CONNECTING EVERYTHING UP

The Raspberry Pi can be used as a traditional computer with a keyboard, mouse and display, or in a headless configuration, where it is accessible on a network and controlled from another computer on the same network. Setting up a Raspberry Pi is a lot easier than you think. As we explained in the previous chapter, it just needs a few easily obtainable cables and a power supply, which could have had a previous life as a mobile phone charger.

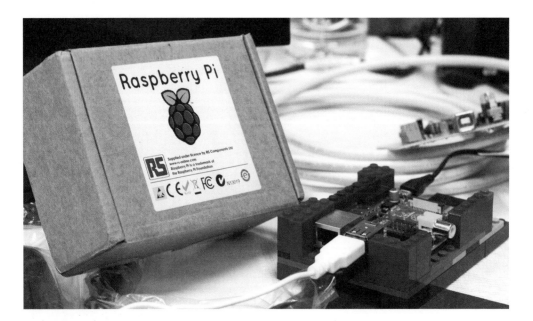

Note on Models

This part of the book assumes that you are setting up the Pi 3B version of the Raspberry Pi. However, the instructions will be almost the same for most models, apart from the Pi Zeros, which have smaller ports and will need adaptors. Although there's also a variation in use of SD or MicroSD cards between newer and older models, we tend to refer to just the 'SD card' to cover everything.

Above: One of the easily obtainable bits of kit you'll need is an HDMI cable.

Keyboard and Mouse

Before powering up, it is best to connect a mouse and keyboard to the USB ports. Then, if using an HDMI lead, connect one end to the HDMI port on your Raspberry Pi, and the other to the display.

If you are using a wireless mouse and keyboard, you only need a single USB port for an RF (radio frequency) or Bluetooth dongle.

Hot Tip

Before going ahead with the set-up, check that you have all necessary components: hardware, cables, display, etc, to hand.

Display

If you are not using a monitor with HDMI, you should connect the Raspberry Pi to an analogue display using the RCA port with an RCA lead. Note that the RCA output is composite video, not RF, so it cannot be attached directly to the antenna input of a TV.

Above: USB port for connecting your mouse and keyboard to the Raspberry Pi.

An RCA to SCART lead connects the computer up to an analogue display. On the Model A+ and B+ Raspberry Pi, the composite video output has been combined with the audio connector, so you need a special cable to allow access to the video output.

Above: Using an RCA cable is an alternative way to connect your Raspberry Pi to a screen.

A few words of caution if you are trying to connect the Raspberry Pi to a VGA monitor: an HDMI to DVI-D (digital) adapter plus a DVI-to-VGA adapter will not work. This is because HDMI does not supply the DVI-A (analogue) needed to convert to VGA. Changing an HDMI or DVI-D source to VGA (or component) needs an active converter – in which case, buying a new monitor may work out cheaper.

Sound

If you are using this analogue configuration, you need to hook up an audio cable between the audio jack on the Raspberry Pi and some speakers. You also need to use an audio lead if your HDMI display doesn't have speakers.

Using a USB Hub

If you expect to use a number of USB peripherals, it's a good idea to insert a USB hub into one of the USB ports in order to extend the number of devices you can plug into the Raspberry Pi. It is also recommended that you use a powered hub, because this supplies any extra power that your devices need, without affecting the Raspberry Pi itself.

Above: A 7-port USB hub for connecting your Raspberry Pi to additional devices.

The USB ports on the Raspberry Pi are fused at about 140 mA each; this is not enough to power something like an external hard drive, and some wireless adapters may struggle to function with that level of power.

Above: Plug your Ethernet cable into the Ethernet port on your Raspberry Pi.

Networking

Insert one end of an Ethernet cable into the Ethernet port on the Raspberry Pi, and the other end into either a router or a wall-mounted Ethernet port that connects up to a network.

SD Card

In the next section, we talk about installing an operating system on to an SD card. Once that is done, you can insert this into the SD card slot just before powering up.

Above: An 8 GB SD card.

Power

It is always best to leave connecting up the Raspberry Pi to the micro USB power supply until last. Although other connections can be made while the unit is switched on, it is good practice to connect these cables while the power is turned off.

If you are using a powered USB hub with your Raspberry Pi, it is a good idea to connect both power supplies to the same switched extension lead, so the powered USB hub and the Raspberry Pi can be switched on and off simultaneously.

If connected to a display, a message should appear when the Raspberry Pi boots. If you are using it in a headless configuration (with no display), when the LEDs have stopped flashing, it should be ready to connect to the Raspberry Pi from another computer via an SSH (secure shell) connection. Operating systems such as Raspbian Linux allow SSH connection by default.

Hot Tip

When powered on for the first time, the Raspberry Pi may take a long time to boot up, so be patient while this happens.

CHOOSING AN OPERATING SYSTEM

The majority of Raspberry Pi operating systems are based around Linux, an open source programming framework. There are many, many flavours of Linux around, but the most common option for Raspberry Pi owners is Rasbian.

When starting out with the Raspberry Pi, most people choose Raspbian as their operating system, but since its launch, many other operating systems have been developed for the tiny computer, all of which can be used for different situations or because they might work in a way that suits you better. Because the operating system runs from an SD card, swapping operating systems is as easy as swapping SD cards. Let's run through the different operating systems that can be used on your Raspberry Pi.

RASPBIAN

Overview

This is the operating system most likely to be installed on the Raspberry Pi. The name is a combination of 'Raspberry' and 'Debian', which

Hot Tip

The open source nature of Linux is that anyone can build their own version of the operating system and make it available to anyone else.

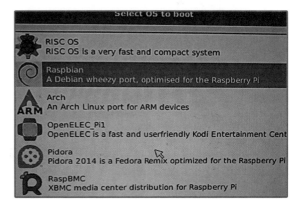

Select OS to boot

RISC OS
RISC OS is a very fast and compact system

Raspbian
A Debian wheezy port, optimised for the Raspberry Pi

Arch
An Arch Linux port for ARM devices

OpenELEC_Pi1
OpenELEC is a fast and userfriendly Kodi Entertainment Cent

Pidora
Pidora 2014 is a Fedora Remix optimized for the Raspberry Pi

RaspBMC
XBMC media center distribution for Raspberry Pi

Above: There are a number of different operating systems that can be set up on the Raspberry Pi.

is the well established Linux-based operating system upon which Raspbian is based. Confusingly, there is also a Debian for Raspberry Pi operating system.

Raspbian comes with free access to over 35,000 software applications and utilities, known as packages, for easy installation on your Raspberry Pi. It is easy to extend and customize the operating system.

Who is it Suitable For?

Raspbian is really aimed at people who are complete beginners but want a proper operating system to start learning to program.

How Do I Get It?

Raspbian can be downloaded from the Raspberry Pi website (www.raspberrypi.org/downloads), and it can also be installed using the NOOBS operating system, which is available from the same place.

Hot Tip

Raspbian is not affiliated with the Raspberry Pi Foundation but has been created by fans of the small computer. While the operating system is free, the developers are always on the lookout for any donations to keep the project going.

UBUNTU

There are two versions of Ubuntu for the Raspberry Pi: Mate and Snappy.

UBUNTU MATE

Overview

This operating system is based on another OS called Ubuntu (also derived from the Debian operating system). This means it gives users a similar desktop experience to that of Windows. Ubuntu Mate is compatible with the ARM7 processor on the Raspberry Pi 3 and Pi 2, but does not work with the original Raspberry Pi. The Mate desktop environment (or user interface) is less resource-hungry than Ubuntu's Unity interface.

Above: The Ubuntu Mate user interface is not dissimilar to that of Windows.

Who is it Suitable For?

Ubuntu Mate is perhaps more suitable for those who are more comfortable with using Ubuntu, or want to develop applications for this operating system. If you use Ubuntu Mate, you won't be able to access software developed to specifically run on Raspbian.

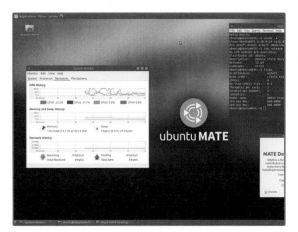

Above: The Ubuntu Mate running on the Raspberry Pi.

How Do I Get It?

Ubuntu Mate can be downloaded via the Raspberry Pi Foundation downloads page (www.raspberrypi.org/downloads).

UBUNTU SNAPPY (AKA UBUNTU CORE)

Overview

Ubuntu Snappy is another Ubuntu distribution, and it has come about as a collaboration between Canonical, the firm behind Ubuntu, and the Raspberry Pi Foundation. It, too, is derived from Debian.

Above: Ubuntu Core is easy to install and once downloaded you can get started with it right away.

Who is it Suitable For?

Also known as Ubuntu Core, it is a lightweight, command line version of the operating system, aimed at developers. It runs on the Raspberry Pi 2 but not the original Raspberry Pi.

Ubuntu Snappy is geared towards building Internet of Things projects on the Raspberry Pi, so is suitable for projects such as home automation, robotics and the like. Applications are self-contained, so when you download them, you don't need to download any other code to get the software up and running.

How Do I Get It?

Ubuntu Snappy (Core) can be downloaded via the Raspberry Pi Foundation downloads page (www.raspberrypi.org/downloads/).

PIDORA

Overview

Pidora is based on yet another Linux operating system, called Fedora. It comes with different software from Raspbian, such as text editors, programming languages and more. It's based on a new build of Fedora for the ARMv6 architecture, with an emphasis on greater speed, and with faster boot-up times.

Above: The Fedora-based operating system Pidora running on Raspberry Pi.

Who is it Suitable For?

More suited to people with intermediate knowledge of operating systems, Pidora also has a headless mode (meaning it can be used without a monitor). But it can still be used as a normal computer with a display attached.

It is also suitable for people who have used the Fedora operating system on normal computers. Pidora itself is clean, simple and very lightweight.

As yet, there isn't as much software for Pidora as there is for Raspbian, but the essentials are there. The software that does exist tends to be more for high-end computers rather than the Raspberry Pi, so this slows things down as well.

How Do I Get It?

Pidora can be downloaded via www.raspberrypi.org/downloads (the Raspberry Pi Foundation downloads page) as part of the NOOBS set-up application.

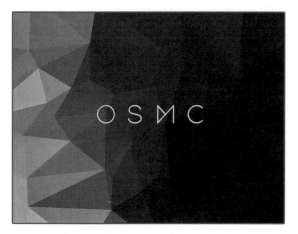

Above: OSMC is a media player based on Linux.

Above: OSMC comes with a settings add-on.

OSMC

Overview

Moving on to operating systems tailored for specific uses, OSMC (Open Source Media Center) is aimed at media centre projects. It is based on Debian Linux and the Kodi Media Center.

Originally known as RaspBMC, it can play all major media formats from a range of devices and streaming protocols. It plays back media from a local network, attached storage and the internet.

Who is it Suitable For?

If you want to tinker with the operating system, OSMC has full access to Debian repositories. It claims that it can be installed in a matter of minutes and receives regular updates.

New apps can be installed via an app store for free, simply by using a remote control that can be bought from OSMC. The app store itself offers things such as a torrent client, web browser and TV tuner.

How Do I Get It?

OSMC can be downloaded via www.raspberrypi.org/downloads (the Raspberry Pi Foundation downloads page) and it can also be found in the NOOBS software package.

RISC OS

Overview

RISC OS has a long pedigree. It was first released way back in 1987 for a distant relative of the Raspberry Pi called Archimedes (after the Greek philosopher and scientist), and is designed to run specifically on ARM processors, which are a central part of the Raspberry Pi. It is a small, light, fast, complete operating system, which takes up less than 10 MB. This makes it able to boot in around 15 seconds. The name comes from RISC, which stands for Reduced Instruction Set Computing, and OS (operating system).

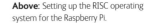

Above: Setting up the RISC operating system for the Raspberry Pi.

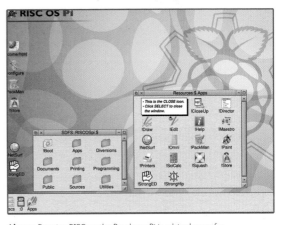

Above: Running RISC on the Raspberry Pi is advised more for intermediate users.

Unlike most other operating systems available for the Raspberry Pi, RISC OS is not based on Linux or any of its distributions.

Who is it Suitable For?

It is not really suitable for beginners. It has networking disabled by default, so you need to read RISC OS Pi's welcome web page (on another machine) to configure the Ethernet port. It comes with a set of applications and utilities, such as a browser, a simple text editor and a scientific calculator, to name just a few. However, if you know the C or C++ programming languages, there is a C/C++ compiler for educational software development, as well as a GCC compiler and Software Development Kit.

How Do I Get It?

The operating system can be installed from the NOOBS distribution, and it is also available from RISC OS Open as a stand-alone version on its own SD card (www.riscosopen. org/content/downloads/raspberry-pi).

ARCH LINUX

Above: Running Arch Linux on the Raspberry Pi for a range of uses.

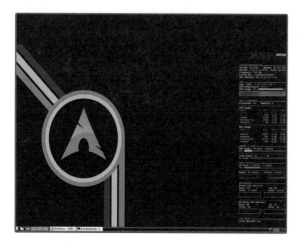

Above: The Arch Linux operating system on the Raspberry Pi.

Overview

As you can probably tell from the name, Arch Linux is another Linux-based operating system, designed for the Raspberry Pi.

Who is it Suitable For?

It is intended for people who are a little more familiar with Linux and intent on learning more. Rather than starting up with a more traditional desktop interface, it starts with an old-fashioned command line interface.

If you want a more user-friendly interface, Arch Linux makes you install it yourself, as well as other software packages and applications. To do this, you need to become proficient in typing commands into a terminal window, rather than opening up a software manager in a window on the desktop.

Updates for the operating system come out whenever they are ready, rather than waiting for a big update every few months.

How Do I Get It?

You can install Arch Linux from the NOOBS set-up software (www.raspberrypi.org/downloads).

OPENELEC

Overview

Another media centre type of operating system, OpenElec can display music, photos and videos from other devices on your network, streamed channels or files from an attached drive, and it enables you to play them back via your monitor or TV.

Above: OpenElec is another versatile operating system styled as a media centre.

While it works on the original Raspberry Pi, OpenElec is far more responsive on the Raspberry Pi 2. It is built around Kodi, the open source media centre; in fact, it is built specifically for the task of running that media player.

Who is it Suitable For?

The operating system itself only takes up around 150–200 MB of space on the SD card, and can boot up in 5–20 seconds, according to the developers. As with OSMC, it is geared towards people who are interested in setting up a media player to connect to their TVs and stream videos, pictures and music.

How Do I Get It?

OpenElec can be downloaded via the Raspberry Pi Foundation downloads page (www. raspberrypi.org/downloads/). It can also be found in the NOOBS software package.

INSTALLING THE OPERATING SYSTEM

While previous versions of the Raspberry Pi used an SD card to hold the operating system, later versions now use a MicroSD card for storage. This means that one of these needs to be prepared for use in your new machine. Having to use an SD card may seem odd, but it does mean that changing the operating system is as easy as changing the SD card.

PREPARE YOUR SD CARD

An SD card can be formatted for use with pre-packaged tools for both Mac and Windows, if it hasn't been formatted already. According to the Raspberry Pi Foundation, a MicroSD card of 8 GB or larger is necessary. Of course, a larger capacity would be more suitable if you intend to use the Raspberry Pi for more data-intensive tasks, such as running a media centre.

Hot Tip

An image file contains compressed versions of many other files. These may also be stored in a folder structure within the image. The image file makes it easier to transfer files and folders to the appropriate places on an SD card. With the files in the right places, the operating system knows where to find them, and this should make starting up the computer an error-free experience.

For the purposes of this book, we are going to look at installing Raspbian on to the Raspberry Pi, but the process is similar for other operating systems. You need another computer with an SD card slot – we are using a Windows PC – to install a file called an image.

Format Your SD Card

Any brand of SD card or MicroSD card (in the case of the Raspberry Pi 2) can be used in a Raspberry Pi. However, before any operating system is put on it, it is best to format it in order to have the maximum capacity available, not only for the operating system but also for any applications you may install later.

A good tool for formatting an SD card is SD Formatter. This is available to download from the SD Association (www.sdcard.org/downloads/formatter_4/).

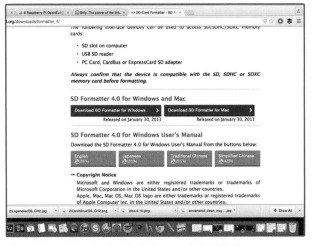

Above: It's possible to download the SD Formatter for both Windows and Mac operating systems.

There are versions for both Windows and Mac. The SD Association recommends using this tool as opposed to generic formatting applications found on Windows and Mac because those tools 'may result in less than optimal performance for your memory cards'.

When SD Formatter has downloaded and installed on your Windows PC or Mac, place the SD card in the SD card slot and click on the Format button. We want to ensure that the maximum capacity of the SD card can be used, so click on Option and ensure Format Size Adjustment is on. Click OK, then click on Format, and click OK again. When finished, the process provides a summary of the card's capacity.

Above: When formatting the SD card, ensure that Format Size Adjustment under 'Format Option' is on.

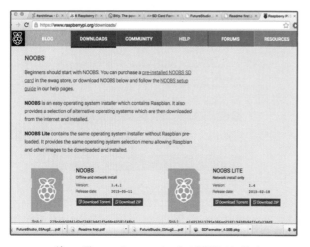

Above: The operating system installer NOOBS is ideal for beginners.

Above: Installing NOOBS.

Download an Image

Now you need to download an image of the operating system. Official images for operating systems can be downloaded from the Raspberry Pi website at www.raspberrypi.org/downloads. As we mentioned earlier, there are many different operating systems, and the Raspberry Pi Foundation recommends most users to download NOOBS, which is designed to make the process of installing an OS as easy as possible. NOOBS stands for New Out Of The Box Software, and it is an easy-to-use operating system installation manager for the Raspberry Pi.

Once the NOOBS zip file has been downloaded, extract the files from the zip file and copy these files on to the SD card you formatted earlier. The files have to be in the root directory of the SD card. If the application you used has extracted files to a folder, you may need to copy the files from inside the folder rather than copy the folder itself, otherwise the card will not boot NOOBS up.

NOOBS has Raspbian included, so it can be installed from the SD card while offline. However, when using NOOBS Lite, or installing any other operating system, you will require an internet connection.

ization size

The operating system image on the full version of NOOBS might have been superseded if a newer version of the OS has been released. However, if connected to the internet, you are given the option of downloading a newer version if there is one.

Install from NOOBS

Once NOOBS has been copied to the SD card, take the card out of the computer you used to format and extract the files to the SD card, and insert it into your Raspberry Pi. Make sure that the keyboard, mouse and monitor cables are plugged in, then power up the Raspberry Pi by plugging the USB power cable into the device.

Above: Copying the files on to the formatted SD card.

> ## Hot Tip
> It is important to note that there are two forms of NOOBS: offline and network install; or network install only.

Start NOOBS on the Raspberry Pi

When booting up for the first time, NOOBS formats your SD card and enables you to select which operating systems you want to install from a list. This list is automatically generated from both locally available OSes (those contained in the /os directory on the card) and those available from a remote repository.

The latest version of each OS is displayed, so you can install the most up-to-date release of the selected OS. The operating systems currently available in NOOBS are Raspbian, Pidora, OpenElec, OSMC, RISC OS and Arch Linux.

Choose Your Operating System

Select the checkbox next to each OS you want to install, using either a mouse or keyboard. Then click the Install icon (or press 'i' on the keyboard) to install the selection.

Hot Tip

There is a built-in web browser (called Arora) which enables you to easily get help via the Raspberry Pi forums. Note that this requires a wired connection to work.

Above: Progress screen for Raspbian installation using NOOBS.

Above: Raspbian is automatically included with NOOBS.

Icons shown on the right of the list indicate whether the OS is being installed from the SD card (SD card icon) or from the online OS repository (Ethernet icon).

Install the Operating System

We are installing Raspbian, so tick the box next to Raspbian and click on Install. Raspbian then runs through its installation process; this may take a while.

Once finished, the Pi configuration menu (raspi-config) loads. Here you can set the time and date for your region, and enable a Raspberry Pi camera board, or even create users. You can exit this menu by using the Tab key on your keyboard to move to Finish.

Log On for the First Time

To log into and access the user interface, you can use the default login for Raspbian – the username is 'pi', and the password is 'raspberry' (without quotes). Type startx to load up the graphical user interface.

On any subsequent boot, you can then press the Shift key to enter the NOOBS interface and easily reinstall your choice of OSes.

THE BOOT PROCESS

What should you expect when you boot up your Raspberry Pi for the first time? The following pages will guide you through the steps to get you set up and even cover some of the more advanced options for those who want them.

GET TO GRIPS WITH RASPI-CONFIG

When the Raspberry Pi is started up for the first time using the Raspbian operating system, it is in set-up mode. If it isn't, you can type the following command to get there:

```
sudo raspi-config
```

This is a command line basic interface, rather than the fancy graphical one. It displays nine options.

When in set-up mode, we can resize the file system to use the entire SD card. This is the first option in the set-up menu.

```
Raspi-config

     info              Information about this tool
     expand_rootfs     Expand root partition to fill SD card
     overscan          Change overscan
     configure_keyboard Set keyboard layout
     change_pass       Change password for 'pi' user
     change_locale     Set locale
     change_timezone   Set timezone
     memory_split      Change memory split
     ssh               Enable or disable ssh server
     boot_behaviour    Start desktop on boot?
     update            Try to upgrade raspi-config


          <Select>                    <Finish>
```

Above: Set-up mode displaying the Raspi-config screen.

```
                    Raspberry Pi Software Configuration Tool (raspi-config)
Setup Options

    1 Expand Filesystem          Ensures that all of the SD card storage is available to the OS
    2 Change User Password       Change password for the default user (pi)
    3 Enable Boot to Desktop/Scratch Choose whether to boot into a desktop environment, Scratch, or the command-line
    4 Internationalisation Options  Set up language and regional settings to match your location
    5 Enable Camera              Enable this Pi to work with the Raspberry Pi Camera
    6 Add to Rastrack            Add this Pi to the online Raspberry Pi Map (Rastrack)
    7 Overclock                  Configure overclocking for your Pi
    8 Advanced Options           Configure advanced settings
    9 About raspi-config         Information about this configuration tool


              <Select>                        <Finish>
```

Above: The nine options available in the Raspberry Pi configuration tool.

Change the User Password

The second option is to change your password. This is generally a good idea if you will be connecting to the internet at some point in the future.

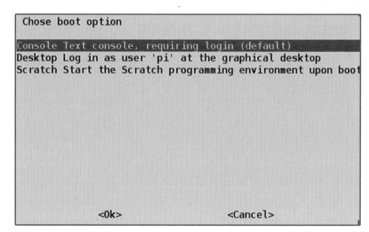

Above: Menu displaying boot options.

Choose How Raspbian Boots Up

The third option enables you to select whether to boot into a desktop environment, Scratch (a programming language – *see* page 74) or the command line interface.

Set the Location, Timezone and Keyboard Options

The next option is Internationalization. Here you can change the locale, for example, en_au.UTF-8 UTF-8 or en_gb.UTF-8 UTF-8. You can also change the timezone. This enables you to update or set the timezone so that it is the correct time for wherever you are. First you select a region – Europe, for example – then choose the city nearest to you.

You can also change the keyboard layout to one that suits the keyboard you are using. Bear in mind that a UK keyboard has a different layout to a US one.

Set Up the Raspberry Pi Camera

The fifth option allows you to enable the Raspberry Pi camera, if you have one. Just select the option and then enable it. This also ensures that there is 128 MB of RAM dedicated for the GPU (graphics processing unit).

Tell Fellow Raspberry Pi Users Where You Are

The Add to Rastrack option adds your Raspberry Pi device to the map of Raspberry Pi users around the world. You can check out Rastrack by heading to www.rastrack.co.uk/.

Speed Up Your Raspberry Pi

The overclock option enables you to get more power out of your Raspberry Pi, although the Pi 3 is less 'overclockable' than older models. The default Raspberry Pi overclock setting is off, and this tool enables you to overclock all flavours of Pi. However, overclocking could potentially shorten the life of your hardware, as well as cause instability.

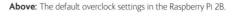

Above: The sixth option lets you add your device details to an online Raspberry Pi user map.

```
Chose overclock preset

None   700MHz ARM, 250MHz core, 400MHz SDRAM, 0 overvolt
Modest 800MHz ARM, 250MHz core, 400MHz SDRAM, 0 overvolt
Medium 900MHz ARM, 250MHz core, 450MHz SDRAM, 2 overvolt
High   950MHz ARM, 250MHz core, 450MHz SDRAM, 6 overvolt
Turbo  1000MHz ARM, 500MHz core, 600MHz SDRAM, 6 overvolt

          <Ok>                    <Cancel>
```

Above: The default overclock settings in the Raspberry Pi 2B.

```
┤ Raspberry Pi Software Configuration Tool (raspi-config) ├
Setup Options

    1 Expand Filesystem          Ensures that all of the SD card storage is available to the OS
    2 Change User Password       Change password for the default user (pi)
    3 Enable Boot to Desktop/Scratch Choose whether to boot into a desktop environment or the command-line
    4 Internationalisation Options  Set up language and regional settings to match your location
    5 Enable Camera              Enable this Pi to work with the Raspberry Pi Camera
    6 Add to Rastrack            Add this Pi to the online Raspberry Pi Map (Rastrack)
    7 Overclock                  Configure overclocking for your Pi
    8 Advanced Options           Configure advanced settings
    9 About raspi-config         Information about this configuration tool

                <Select>                                    <Finish>
```

Above: Selecting Advanced Options from the menu.

MORE ADVANCED OPTIONS

Raspi-config also offers Advanced Options for more advanced users.

Adjust the Display

The first sub-option is called Overscan. If your display has a black border around it, you have underscan. But if the display is too big for the monitor, you have overscan. This option, when enabled, helps fix display problems.

```
What would you like to do with overscan




                <Disable>          <Enable>
```

Above: Fix display problems using the overscan option.

Change the Pi's Name on the Network

Hostname enables you to set the Raspberry Pi's network name.

Change Memory to Suit Your Needs

Memory Split enables you to change the amount of memory available to the GPU. You can make this larger or smaller, depending on what you're planning on doing with the Pi.

Allow Remote Access

SSH enables you to disable/enable SSH access to your Raspberry Pi. Switching this on enables you to access your Pi from a remote location. If you don't plan on ever using this, it is best to keep it disabled. If you're also planning on using it on a public network, make sure that all passwords have been changed, so they are stronger.

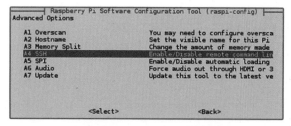

Above: Enable or Disable remote access to your device using this option.

Enable the Pi to Interact with External Sensors

SPI enables the Serial Peripheral Interface kernel module, which is needed by the PiFace interface, to be turned on and off. It enables you to connect a four-wire serial link, so you have sensors, memory and peripherals.

I2C is the sub-option to enable or disable the 2C kernel module, so you're able to connect I2C devices.

Serial toggles shell and kernel messages from the serial connection on and off.

Above: A Raspberry Pi in use.

Enable Sound

Audio enables you to force audio out of either the 3.5 mm jack or the HDMI port. By default, this is set to Auto, which means it automatically determines which output to send sound through.

Update

Finally, there is the option to download and install the latest version of the raspi-config tool.

Save Your Settings

Once you are done with using this tool, choose Finish. You are asked whether you would like to reboot or stay on the command line. It is usually best to reboot, so that all the changes can be applied.

RASPBERRY PI & PROGRAMMING

PROGRAMMING BASICS

The original and most important purpose of the Raspberry Pi is to teach people about technology and how to program a computer.

In this chapter, we look at the basics of programming and give a brief overview of two of the most popular programming languages you can learn on Raspbian (the recommended version of Linux for the Raspberry Pi). These languages are Scratch and Python. Scratch is aimed at people who are new to computer programming, particularly children, whereas Python is more advanced but still easy enough for anyone to grasp the basics.

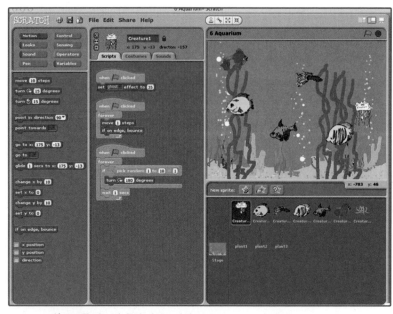

Above: The Scratch Studio, here with the Aquarium project loaded.

WHAT IS A PROGRAM?

Before we look at Scratch and Python, we need to explain some of the jargon that comes with programming.

A program is a set of repeatable instructions to make a computer, such as the Raspberry Pi, do something. Such instructions can be very complex because they

have to go into a lot
of detail about what a
computer needs to do
when carrying out these
instructions.

Programming can be
done on any platform;
a platform being
a combination of
hardware and software.
In this instance, the
Raspberry Pi is the
hardware and the
Raspbian operating
system is the software.

Above: An overview of the programming language Python.

Programming is not only a science, it is also an art, and programs can be created in many
ways, using many different languages.

Choosing the Right Language

Different languages have
different ways of creating
instructions for the computer
to follow. As such, they are
suited for different tasks. Scratch
is good for learning what
programming is all about and
can be used to create simple
games and animations.

Above: The Scratch logo.

If you need to create something more complex, such as a mathematical program, Python is more suitable. However, creating programs with Python takes longer because it is more powerful and has more flexibility.

Above: The Python logo.

MASTERING PROGRAMMING

Understanding a language isn't the be-all and end-all of programming – understanding the control and data structures, as well as the design of a program, is what really matters. All programming languages, even Scratch, have elements that are common to other languages; these help you to learn how to put a program together. So decide what type of programming you want to do and use a language that works for you.

In order to program a computer, you need to write instructions in a language (rules), and these instructions need to achieve your desired results (logic). Think of it as following a few tasks in a certain way. For instance, your nightly routine might be that you always first brush your teeth, then change your clothes and finally get into bed. You need to follow these steps in a certain order to achieve the result: getting a good night's sleep. If you can think through the order in which things must happen, you can program.

Hot Tip

After writing and compiling, you need to test your program to see whether it does things the way you want. If not, you need to re-write the program. This is called debugging.

One thing a computer can't do (well, not yet) is read your mind. A computer only does what you tell it to do. If your program doesn't do what you want, you must have forgotten to tell it something, or else told it the wrong thing. This may seem obvious, but you need to keep it in mind when you think about creating a computer program.

HOW TO PROGRAM

There are essentially two steps to programming: writing and compiling.

Writing involves breaking down the program into step-by-step instructions. Sometimes writing this out on paper first can help (this is known as pseudocode). When writing longer programs, mapping things out on paper is invaluable. Once the steps have been figured out, you can write the program in the language you choose.

The next step is compiling the program. The compiler is a piece of software that takes what you have written in text form on a computer, and translates this into a form the machine can understand and carry out.

```
#This is my adventure game

def scene1():
    print('You are standing on a trail in a forrest')
    print('Before you the trail splits in two')
    print('Which way will you go right or left?','\n')

def makeChoice():
    choice = ''
    while choice != '1' and choice != '2':
        print('Press 1 followed by enter to choose the first option')
        print('Press 2 followed by enter to choose the second option')
        choice = input()
    return choice

def scene2A():
    print('You come to a stream with bridge')
    print('You can cross and follow the trail that leads from the bridge')
    print('or follow the trail that leads along the nearside of the river','\n'

def scene2B():
    print('you come to a steep hill')
    print('you can climb over the hill')
    print('or you can follow the trail which leads around it','\n')

#main program starts here
scene1()

#use the makeChoice function to get the player to decide which way to go
firstChoice  = makeChoice()
```

Above: Writing steps out in pseudocode is a handy way of working through what you want to do before translating it fully into computing language.

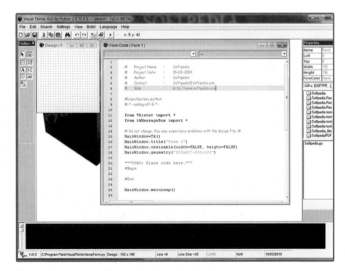

Above: A program compiler translates the written code.

PROGRAMMING IN SCRATCH

The Raspberry Pi was created in part to encourage children – the next generation of developers – to create programs, and Scratch is a perfect environment in which kids can learn the basics of programming. It can be used to create cartoons and games, and by doing this, people learning Scratch find out about the concepts used by professionals.

Scratch has been developed so that anyone can use it. It has a graphical interface, which makes it easy to see what you can do without having to remember vast amounts of code, and you can quickly make successful applications. In many cases, you barely even need to use a keyboard to create a basic program.

Above: Children are becoming more in tune with programming.

BUILDING A SCRATCH PROGRAM

Developed by MIT's Media Lab, Scratch works a little like a jigsaw puzzle, in that graphical blocks of code can be fitted together to create a complete, working program. This technique is called block scripting, and it means you don't need to use an editor and symbolic language to create your own code, which would be more complicated.

The integrated development environment is called Scratch Studio. This includes everything you need to develop full applications. It comes with a load of example projects, pictures and sounds to help a newbie get started.

Hot Tip

All Scratch applications can run on Windows, Mac or Linux, or can be shared online.

USING SCRATCH STUDIO

Scratch comes pre-installed on Raspbian. With Scratch, you can make animations and games without having to learn a complicated programming language, and you will pick up the concepts of programming along the way.

Scratch 1.4 comes installed on the 'Wheezy' Raspbian operating systems – you should find either an icon on the desktop or an item in the desktop menu.

To begin programming in Scratch, click on the cat icon for Scratch Studio on the desktop or find it in the desktop menu.

FIND YOUR WAY AROUND

Scratch Studio itself is divided into four panels, each with its own job to do. Located at the top of the window are the menu and three quick access icons.

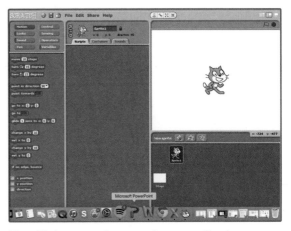

Above: Open the Scratch app by clicking on the cat icon.

Above: The home screen that appears when you open Scratch.

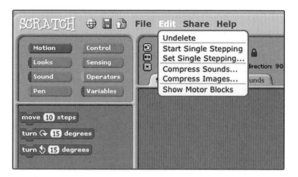

Above: The file tab in Scratch.

Above: The edit tab in Scratch.

Above: The share tab in Scratch.

Menu Options

- **File:** Here you can open, save and import projects based on Scratch. The Project Notes option enables you to describe the project and make notes.

- **Edit:** This contains a variety of tools to help with editing animations, images and sounds.

- **Share:** Pretty much self-explanatory, this option enables you to share your projects with others worldwide. A Scratch project can be posted on Scratch's community website via the Share This Project Online option and the Upload To Scratch Server form.

- **Help:** This is your gateway to help pages on the internet, should you get stuck and need more information.

Quick Access

The quick access icons help you to set language options, save projects and share them.

The Stage

The Stage is where the program runs and the action happens. This Stage consists of images known as sprites. At the top-right you can see a green flag and a red circle. The flag starts the program, while the circle stops it.

Located above the flag and circle are three buttons that control the viewing mode. The two buttons on the left increase and decrease the size of the Stage. The final button, on the right, is used for Presentation Mode, which displays the program full screen. If you want to stop full-screen mode, simply press the Escape key on your keyboard.

Underneath the Stage is the Sprite List. Sprites are like game characters, there to do your bidding. When you start up, you'll see a sprite of a cat.

GETTING STARTED

A Scratch program can be created simply by putting blocks together. The panel on the left is called the Blocks Palette. Each block in here represents short instructions to make your sprites move – for instance, move 10 steps, rotate 15 degrees left or right, or point in a specific direction.

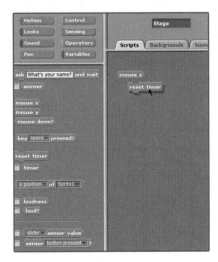

You can drag and drop a sprite anywhere on the Stage, as well as increase or decrease its size by clicking on it. The mouse pointer changes to arrows pointing outwards (for making sprites bigger) or inwards (for making sprites smaller).

The middle panel is the Scripts area, where your program is created. You assemble the blocks simply by dragging them into this area from the Blocks Palette. When the blocks are assembled, they tell the sprite to move, change direction or rotate.

Above: Drag blocks into the Scripts area to program a function in Scratch.

PROGRAMMING IN PYTHON

Python is an extremely powerful, dynamic, open source programming language used in a wide variety of applications.

```
#!/usr/bin/env python2.7
# by Alex Eames of http://RasPi.TV

import RPi.GPIO as GPIO
import sys, os
from time import sleep

GPIO.setmode(GPIO.BCM)                    # initialise RPi.GP
GPIO.setup(25, GPIO.OUT)              # set up ports for output

answer = raw_input("Are you sure you want to reset? y/n \n")

if answer != "y" and answer != "yes":
    print "OK. Not resetting. To change your mind, rerun the program"
    GPIO.cleanup()
    sys.exit()

try:
    print "OK. Syncing file system, then resetting."
    command = os.system("sync")
    if command == 0:
        print "sync successful - resetting now"
        sleep(1)
        GPIO.output(25, 1)
        sleep(10)
        GPIO.output(25, 0)
        print "I think you forgot to connect your wires. Connect them up an
        GPIO.cleanup()

except KeyboardInterrupt:              # trap a CTRL+C keyboard interrupt
    GPIO.cleanup()
```

Above: An example of some basic Python programming.

It is often compared to other powerful programming languages, such as Ruby, Perl, Java and C++. All in all, Python is a great language to start with and you can get instant results.

It is also one of the main languages used on the Raspberry Pi. It is stable and mature, so it has very few bugs in it. This is because Python has relatively few lines of code, making it less prone to problems, easier to debug and more maintainable.

WHY USE PYTHON?

Python is an excellent language to use if you are a beginner, but it is also complex enough for experts. Within an hour, you can easily understand how a piece of Python code runs; it is simple and elegant.

It is also highly scalable – in other words, it is suitable for small projects as well as very large ones. In fact, it powers most of YouTube and Dropbox. Even Google has made Python one of its official programming languages.

Above: Dropbox, Google and YouTube all use Python programming.

Python is portable and cross-platform, too. This means that projects developed to run on a Raspberry Pi could also run on other platforms, such as Windows, Mac and Linux. It can also be embedded into hardware.

Because it is a mature language, it boasts a number of powerful, standard libraries of pre-built code and sub-routines to help you get your projects up and running in next to no time. It is also installed by default on Raspbian.

THE BUILDING BLOCKS OF PYTHON

Now we are going to look at creating our own programs with Python. As we mentioned, it is easy to learn, while being powerful enough to create interesting programs. Before creating these programs,

though, we need to look at the basic building blocks and concepts of Python.

Python Doesn't Need to Compile

Unlike a lot of languages, Python doesn't need to compile code before running, because it's what's known as an interpreted language. You can run the program as soon as you make changes to the file, which makes revising and troubleshooting programs much quicker than in many other languages.

Try Things Out in the Interpreter

The interpreter can be used to test code without having to add it to the rest of your program. This helps you to learn how commands work.

Above: The Python interpreter window.

Handling Objects and Variables

Variables are a data item that may take on more than one value during the runtime of a program. An object can be a variable, a data structure or a function – or a combination of any or all three. Python is object-oriented, which means that everything within a program is regarded as an object. Variables do not need to be declared at the start of the program but can be declared at any time. Not only that, but you don't need to specify variable types.

Above: Locate the development environment IDLE under Applications.

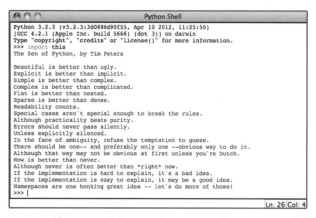

Above: Writing Python in IDLE is an easy way of familiarizing yourself with Python programming.

Using IDLE

The easiest way to learn how to program in Python is by using IDLE, a Python development environment. This is already installed on Raspbian, and can be opened from the Desktop or Applications menu in the operating system.

IDLE features what is known as a REPL (Read-Evaluate-Print-Loop) prompt, so you can enter Python commands directly into the editor.

Creating Files in IDLE

To create a file in IDLE, click File, then New File. This opens up a blank window, which is an empty file rather than a prompt. A Python file can be written here. If you save and run it, you see its output in the other window.

BASIC USE

Now we are ready to use our first command. As with all good programming books, we are going to start by printing the phrase 'Hello World'. The code required is very simple:

```
Print ("Hello World").
```

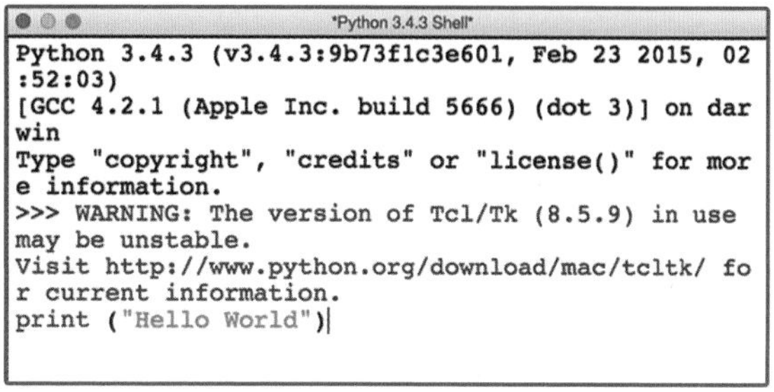

Making an Indent

Curly braces – {} – are used by some computer languages to wrap around lines of code that belong together, leaving the writer to indent the lines if they wish, so you can see at a glance that they are nested. However, indentation is mandatory for nesting in Python. For example:

```
For I in range(10):
        Print ("Hello World")
```

Indenting is necessary here. If a second line is indented, it becomes part of the loop.

```
for i in range(2):
        print("Hello")
        print("World")
```

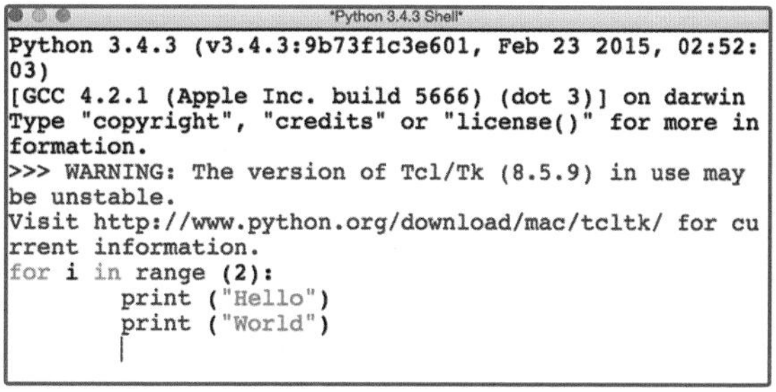

This would print:

Hello

World

Hello

World

Above: A first attempt at programming using Python.

Above: Making an indent in Python.

Above: Indenting a second line.

However, if we typed this:

```
for i in range(2):
    print("Hello")
print("World")
```

We would get this:

Hello

Hello

World

```
Python 3.4.3 (v3.4.3:9b73f1c3e601, Feb 23 201
5, 02:52:03)
[GCC 4.2.1 (Apple Inc. build 5666) (dot 3)] o
n darwin
Type "copyright", "credits" or "license()" fo
r more information.
>>> WARNING: The version of Tcl/Tk (8.5.9) in
use may be unstable.
Visit http://www.python.org/download/mac/tclt
k/ for current information.
name ="Bill"
>>> age= 20|
```

Above: Assigning values to variables.

Variables

We can assign values to variables. For example:

```
name = "Bill"
age = 20
```

Types are not assigned to variables, however. These are inferred and can be changed, because they are dynamic.

```
Age = 20
Age += 2 # increment age by 2
Print(age)
```

Comments

Comments are notes you can make to explain what is happening in the program. They are denoted by the hash symbol (#), as seen in the above example. If you have comments that run on for more than one line, triple quotes are used at the beginning and the end:

```
" " "
This is a Python program that
prints "Hello World".
That is all!
" " "

print("Hello World")
```

Lists

Also known as arrays in some languages, lists collate data of any type. Square brackets are used around the list, and the items are separated by commas:

```
numbers = [2, 4, 6]
```

Iteration

Python has what is known as `for` loops. They don't need to be used very much, though, because Python is good at doing things in other ways. Other languages don't have list types like Python does, which means that a lot of manual work needs to be done instead, such as specifying starts, ends and steps to define integer or character ranges. In Python, a `for` loop iterates over a list:

```
list = ['a', 'b', 'c']
        for letter in list:
        print letter

a
b
c
```

```
Python 3.4.3 Shell
Python 3.4.3 (v3.4.3:9b73f1c3e601, Feb 23 2015, 02:52:03)
[GCC 4.2.1 (Apple Inc. build 5666) (dot 3)] on darwin
Type "copyright", "credits" or "license()" for more information
.
>>> WARNING: The version of Tcl/Tk (8.5.9) in use may be unstab
le.
Visit http://www.python.org/download/mac/tcltk/ for current inf
ormation.
range (4)
range(0, 4)
>>> [0,1,2,3]
[0, 1, 2, 3]
>>>
```

Above: A list of numbers.

```
*Python 3.4.3 Shell*
Python 3.4.3 (v3.4.3:9b73f1c3e601, Feb 23 2015, 02:52
:03)
[GCC 4.2.1 (Apple Inc. build 5666) (dot 3)] on darwin
Type "copyright", "credits" or "license()" for more i
nformation.
>>> WARNING: The version of Tcl/Tk (8.5.9) in use may
be unstable.
Visit http://www.python.org/download/mac/tcltk/ for c
urrent information.
list= ['a','b','c']
```

Above: Programming a 'for' loop.

```
Python 3.4.3 Shell
Python 3.4.3 (v3.4.3:9b73f1c3e601, Feb 23 2015, 02:52:03)
[GCC 4.2.1 (Apple Inc. build 5666) (dot 3)] on darwin
Type "copyright", "credits" or "license()" for more information
.
>>> WARNING: The version of Tcl/Tk (8.5.9) in use may be unstab
le.
Visit http://www.python.org/download/mac/tcltk/ for current inf
ormation.
range (4)
range(0, 4)
>>> [0,1,2,3]
[0, 1, 2, 3]
>>> |
```

Above: Creating a list of integers.

Range

The built-in range function can be used to create a list of integers:

```
range(4)
[0, 1, 2, 3]


range(3, 6)
[3, 4, 5]


range(2, 10, 3)
[2, 5, 8]
```

Length

The built-in len function can be used to find the length of a list:

```
List  = [1, 2, 3, 4]
len(a)
4
```

If Statements

An if statement can be used to control the flow of a program. It is a condition that, when fulfilled, triggers another part of the code. It is often combined with else if and else.

```
a = 10
if a == 12:
        print("if")
elif a == 11:
        print("elif")
else:
        print("else")
```

The elif statement enables you to check multiple expressions for being true, and executes a block of code as soon as one of the conditions is true.

Similar to else, the elif statement is optional. However, unlike else, for which there can be only one statement at most, there can be any number of elif statements following an if.

SCRATCH PROJECTS

The best way to learn a programming language is to write a program, so have a go at the following projects using Scratch.

CAT DANCING

1. One of the first projects you can try out is to make the Scratch cat do a little dance. Open up Scratch on the Raspberry Pi by clicking on the Scratch icon.

2. Now start moving the blocks shown in the picture. The numbers in the instructions can be changed by clicking on them and typing in the desired figure.

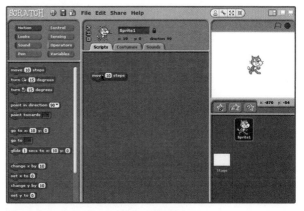

Above: Programming the cat to dance in Scratch.

3. This simple program teaches us a few concepts about how programming works. First, sequence is important – move the blocks around and the cat dances in a different way.

4. Second, a loop makes the program go on for ever (unless you hit the Stop button). The instructions within the for loop will just keep going and going.

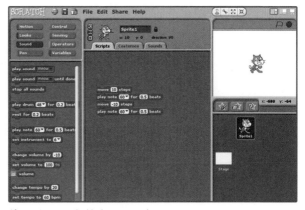

Above: Arranging the blocks programs the cat to move in a certain way.

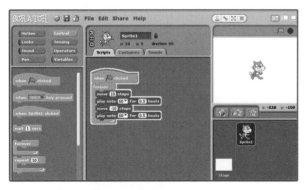

Above: Adding a control event.

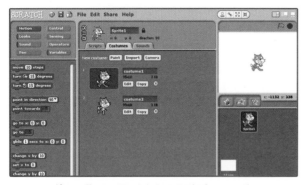

Above: Change sprite costumes using the Costumes tab.

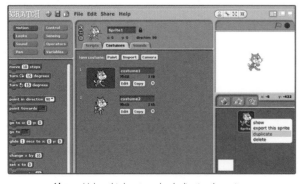

Above: Make a third costume by duplicating the sprite.

5. Third, a control event triggers the program. In this instance, the cat starts dancing 'When Green Flag Clicked'. This is a command to run the Scratch program.

CHANGE THE LOOK OF A SPRITE

1. Sprites in Scratch can 'wear' different costumes. To change their appearance, simply click on a sprite to select it, then click on the Costumes tab. The cat has two costumes; to make a third one, right-click on the sprite and choose Duplicate.

2. Choose Costume3 and click on Edit. This opens the Paint Editor. There are lots of buttons and options that enable you to change the look of the sprite's costume. Draw on the sprite and click OK.

3. You can then switch between costumes by adding the purple Looks block called Next Costume to the loop you made in the previous project. Now run your program to see the sprite change costumes before your very eyes.

CHANGE BACKGROUND, ADD SPRITES AND MAKE THEM JUMP

1. You can change the backdrop of a Scratch window very easily. Underneath the Stage, next to the Sprites window, is a small box named Stage. Click on that, then on the Backdrops tab.

2. Change the backdrop by clicking on the Choose Backdrop From Library icon. Select a picture, then click OK. You can also design your own backdrop by either using the paint tools, uploading your own picture, or even using the camera on your computer to take a selfie.

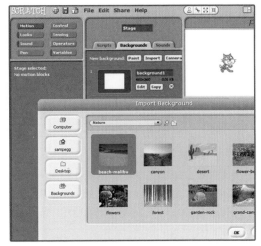

Above: You can change the background in Scratch by importing or uploading a new image.

3. Sprites can be changed just as easily. Click on a Sprites box underneath the Stage window, then click on the 'New Sprite' button at the top. You can design a new sprite by clicking on the paintbrush symbol next to the New Sprite symbol.

4. You can make your new sprite jump whenever you click on it.

MAKE A GAME OF PONG

Now we're going to make a very basic game of Pong. First, create a new project, then choose the background of the game, as before. In this case, we have chosen the Underwater3 backdrop.

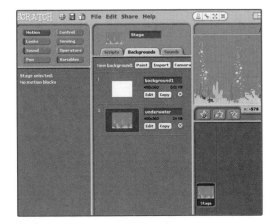

Above: Selecting an underwater background for a new project.

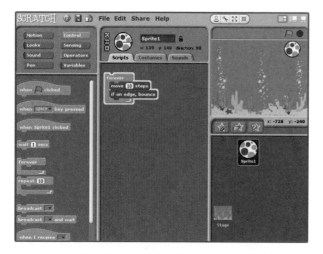

Step 2: Apply Motion and Control blocks for the moving ball.

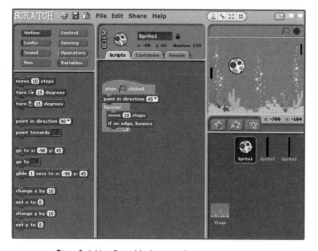

Step 1: Add an Event block to give the program a starting point.

Add Sprites

1. Next we need to add two sprites: a ball and a paddle. These are stock sprites that come within Scratch. Click on the Sprites window, locate the relevant sprites, then click on the New Sprite icon to add them to the program.

2. Now we have to make the ball move. Click on the ball and drag it to the top of the Stage, where it will start. Then click on the Motion category and drag a Move block on to the Scripts area. We need to keep the ball moving, so snap on a block called If On Edge, Bounce. Click on the Control category and wrap a Forever block around the other blocks.

3. When you click on the stack of blocks, the ball moves, but only from side to side. We need to make it move around the Stage. To make it go at an angle, drag a Point In Direction block on top of the Forever block. Type in an angle, such as 45 degrees.

Add Events

1. Now click on the Event category and drag a block called When Green Flag Clicked.

You can change the speed of the ball by changing the number of steps the ball takes in the Move X Steps block.

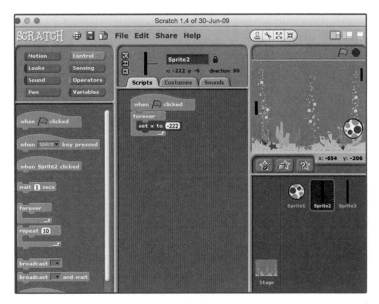

Step 2: Set the program for the paddle (sprite 2) using Motion and Control blocks.

2. The next thing to do is move the paddle. Go to the Motion category and choose Set X To (you can set X to follow the x co-ordinate of the mouse, by dragging a Mouse block from the Sensing category on to this block). Wrap a Forever block around that (from the Control category). Then, from the Events category, drag a When Green Flag Clicked block over on top of the Forever block.

3. To get the ball to bounce off the paddle, choose the ball sprite and add this to the script. Choose When Green Flag Clicked from Events, then Forever from the Control category. Within the Forever loop, drag an If...Then block and place that inside the Forever loop.

4. Drag a Touching block from the Sensing category on to the If...Then block. Select Paddle from the drop-down menu, then drag in a Turn Clockwise (a clockwise icon) X Degrees block from the Motion category. Enter 180 degrees. Then drag a Wait 1 Secs block and place that underneath the Turn 180 Degrees block. To add a sound that plays every time the paddle hits the ball, drag a Play Sound Pop block from the Sound category into the If...Then block.

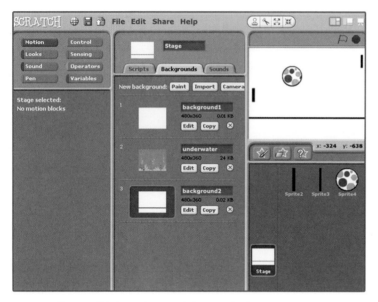

Add a Challenge

Time to add a challenge. Select the Stage, then the Backdrops Tab. Select the line tool and draw a thick line at the bottom (holding down the Shift key while drawing the line makes it straight).

Select the ball sprite and add a script to make the ball stop if it hits the line colour. Drag the When Green Flag Clicked block from the Events category on to the script for the ball.

Above: Add the bounce line using the Backgrounds tab.

Then drag the Forever block from the Control category underneath that. Now place an If...Then block within the Forever block. Drag a Touching Color block from the Sensing category, then click inside the square box within this block. Now move your cursor to point and click on the bottom line colour.

MAKE SOMETHING ARTISTIC

Scratch can also be used to make artistic patterns, such as spirals. For this project, it doesn't matter which sprite you use because it will be hidden.

Making a Spiral

We want a spiral to be drawn whenever we click on a mouse button. To do this, add the script blocks for the sprite as described here:

The main block drives the program. When the green flag is clicked, it sets the pen size and hides it. It also sets a user-created variable, called Distance, to zero. To create this variable, click on the Data category, then click on Make a Variable. It asks you to type in a name – in this case, type distance.

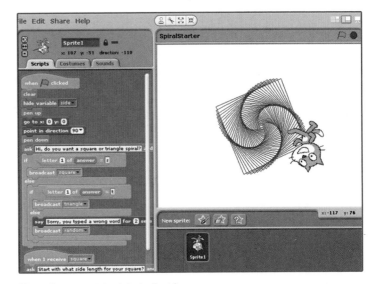

Above: Create an artistic spiral using Scratch.

The next part of the main block is a Forever loop. Here, when the program detects a mouse click (as part of an If...Then block), it starts another program block to draw the actual spiral. Click on the More Blocks category and call this program block Draw a Spiral.

This is very much like a sub-routine in a normal program. The Draw a Spiral sub-routine begins to make a spiral from where it detected a mouse click on the Stage. It starts drawing from a random angle, then a Repeat block loops a set number of times (in this case 300), changing colour, adding a bit more to the distance the pen has to travel, drawing a small line equal to the new distance variable, adjusting the angle slightly, then repeating.

After the set number of loops, it resets the distance variable to zero, and waits until the mouse has been clicked before doing the same thing over again.

This project teaches you about the concept of modules in the programming language. While everything could have been written as one large block, splitting it up into smaller blocks makes the project easier to read, understand and maintain, which is good programming practice.

PYTHON PROJECTS

Once you have got to grips with Scratch, you may want to move on to Python, especially if you want to tackle more in-depth and serious projects with the Raspberry Pi.

As we've already mentioned, Python is not just for educational projects, but it has commercial uses, too. So let's have a look at some projects for the Raspberry Pi that you can program with Python.

WHAT YOU NEED

You should already have your Raspberry Pi set up with Raspbian installed. We are going to use an application called IDLE to help create our applications. IDLE is known as an integrated development environment, or IDE. An IDE is used to create programs and applications.

Above: The Python logo.

IDLE is both a console and an editor – as we type in Python commands, IDLE interprets what we write and carries out these commands.

Hot Tip

There are two main versions of Python: Python 2 and Python 3. Python 3 is the newest version, but Python 2 is included with the Raspberry Pi. Version 2.7 is the latest, most stable release of Python 2, and when an upgrade to Python 3 is available for the Raspberry Pi, installing it should be straightforward.

EVERYTHING NEAT AND TIDY

Python code is neat. If you have used another programming language, such as JavaScript or PHP, you might notice the lack of curly braces that usually enclose sections of code. This is because Python uses indentation to organize the code you write.

This is good practice in any language, but it is mandatory in Python. If the spacing isn't right, the code won't work.

```
 IDLE  File  Edit  Shell  Debug  Options  Window  Help
                  Python 3.4.3 Shell
Python 3.4.3 (v3.4.3:9b73f1c3e601, Feb 23 2015, 02
:52:03)
[GCC 4.2.1 (Apple Inc. build 5666) (dot 3)] on dar
win
Type "copyright", "credits" or "license()" for mor
e information.
>>> WARNING: The version of Tcl/Tk (8.5.9) in use
may be unstable.
Visit http://www.python.org/download/mac/tcltk/ fo
r current information.
range10
Traceback (most recent call last):
  File "<pyshell#0>", line 1, in <module>
     range10
NameError: name 'range10' is not defined
>>> |
```

Above: If the code isn't spaced correctly in Python it won't work.

OBJECT ORIENTATION

Another concept to get your head around is object-oriented programming. Python is a simple representation of the idea. It is a difficult concept to grasp and define, but it's a way of programming that is based on objects, and it uses these objects to build and design applications. In other words, you have an object, you define what the object is (give it characteristics), then you tell that object what to do.

Python is not too fussy when it comes to how variables or objects are created or managed, which makes it very productive.

GETTING USED TO PYTHON
Create Your First Program
Open up IDLE on the Raspbian desktop, and you can start to program in Python. In a new window, type the following: >>> print "Hello World!"

This is a very popular basic program, which prints 'Hello World' on the screen. IDLE immediately compiles whatever you have typed. This is useful for testing things, such as defining a few variables, then checking to see whether a certain line works.

```
Python 3.4.3 (v3.4.3:9b73f1c3e601, Feb 2
3 2015, 02:52:03)
[GCC 4.2.1 (Apple Inc. build 5666) (dot
3)] on darwin
Type "copyright", "credits" or "license(
)" for more information.
>>> WARNING: The version of Tcl/Tk (8.5.
9) in use may be unstable.
Visit http://www.python.org/download/mac
/tcltk/ for current information.
print ("hello, world")
hello, world
>>> |
```

Above: A very basic Python program.

Calculation in Python

Python can also carry out calculations. Try the following examples.

```
Python 3.4.3 (v3.4.3:9b73f1c3e601, Feb 23 2015
, 02:52:03)
[GCC 4.2.1 (Apple Inc. build 5666) (dot 3)] on
darwin
Type "copyright", "credits" or "license()" for
more information.
>>> WARNING: The version of Tcl/Tk (8.5.9) in
use may be unstable.
Visit http://www.python.org/download/mac/tcltk
/ for current information.
1 + 1
2
>>> 20 + 100
120
>>> 18295+449566
467861
>>> 10-5
5
>>> 3*3
9
>>> 3**2
9
>>> 21/3
7.0
>>>
```

Above: Python can calculate exponentials.

Addition

```
>>> 1 + 1
2
>>> 20+100
120
>>> 18295+449566
467861
```

Subtraction

```
>>>10-5
5
```

Multiplication

```
>>>3*3
9
```

You can even calculate exponentials (squares, cubes and so on):

```
>>>3**2
9
```

Division

Here's where things get a little more complicated.

```
>>> 21/3
7
```

That was simple enough, but what about this?

```
>>> 23/3
7
```

That's nearly right but all Python did was output a whole number. Type:

```
>>> 23.0/3.0
7.6666...
```

Now we get a more accurate answer because we have specified outputting after the decimal point.

Adding Comments

When your programs get more complicated, you might want to add an explanation of what is happening at a certain point in the program. However, you don't want Python to interpret your comment as a command. Adding the hash (#) symbol is a little like adding a hashtag in Twitter – it encapsulates your thoughts about something.

```
>>># This is a very simple
program
>>>print "Hello World"
Hello World
```

Here only 'Hello World' is printed out. Anything in the comments stays in the comments.

```
Python 3.4.3 Shell
Python 3.4.3 (v3.4.3:9b73f1c3e601, Feb 23 2015, 02:52:03)
[GCC 4.2.1 (Apple Inc. build 5666) (dot 3)] on darwin
Type "copyright", "credits" or "license()" for more information.
>>> WARNING: The version of Tcl/Tk (8.5.9) in use may be unstable.
Visit http://www.python.org/download/mac/tcltk/ for current informati
23.0/3.0
7.666666666666667
>>>
```

Above: Producing a decimal point answer in IDLE.

PROGRAMMING IN A FILE

IDLE is great but when you want to write multiple lines of code, using a simple text editor is a good idea. Either Leafpad on Raspbian or the widely used VIM are more than up to the job. The text editor doesn't try to run your Python program, so you can add as many lines as you want, then save them to run in IDLE.

Open a new file in Leafpad and on the first line type:

```
#!/usr/bin/python
```

This tells the operating system that it will use Python, in the folder /usr/bin/, to run the file. This needs to be added to all Python programs.

```
[No Name] + - VIM
#!/usr/bin/python
```

Above: The command screen of the text editor VIM.

Next, type in this line:

```
name = raw_input('What is
your name? ')
```

```
[No Name] + - VIM
name = raw_input('What is your name? ')
```

Above: Creating a variable name.

This creates a variable, name, and displays the question, 'What is your name?' The user types in their name and the program stores the result. The inverted commas tell the computer that this is a single piece of text. We can then use this variable to make a print statement more personal. Type in the following:

```
Print 'Hello', name
```

You have to type these lines in the correct order, because the program displays an error if we print the variable before we have created it.

Now save the file as `hello.py`, open up a Terminal window (this is where you tell the Raspberry Pi to run your commands), and type in `chmod a+x hello.py`. This tells your Raspberry Pi that the file is executable and can be run as a program.

Above: Save the file.

Above: Open a Terminal window in order to see the output of your saved command.

Above: Setting up an 'If...then' function.

Next type `./hello.py` at the Terminal prompt to run the program. It asks you to type in your name and then personally greets you.

ADD DECISIONS

While this program sets up variables and acts on them, it is a little limited. You can add an `if...then` statement to allow you to make a decision about the content of a variable and act on it. It is just like the If...Then block we looked at in Scratch.

The basic structure of an `if...then` statement looks like this:

```
if <expression> :
<indent> code block
```

The expression must be something that can be either true or false, so we can add this statement after the 'What is your name?' line in the program:

```
If name=='Holly' :
```

We put Holly in inverted commas so the computer knows this is text. The colon tells the computer that this If... is finished and we are about to tell it what to do next. What do we do next? We greet the person!

```
If name=='Holly' :
    Print 'hi', name, " you're an awesome individual!"
```

```
Execute    main.py
1  #!/usr/bin/python
2~ If name=='Holly':
3    Print 'hi', name, " you're an awesome individual!"
```

Above: In order to complete the 'If...then' function, add a result for when the 'If' criteria is met.

```
Execute    main.py
1  #!/usr/bin/python
2  name = raw_input (What is your name ? ')
3~ If name=='Holly':
4    Print 'hi', name, " you're an awesome individual!"
5~   else :
6    print 'Hello', name
```

Above: Add an 'Else' function for when the 'If' criteria is not met.

Hot Tip

The double equals sign (==) is there to prevent vagueness when it comes to programming. We use a single equals (=) when assigning values to variables, so we need something else to check is something is equal to something else, hence the double equals sign.

There are a couple of spaces at the start of the second line to indent it, because we are going to write a few lines within this block of code (indents are needed in Python). We also use double speech marks here, because it encloses an apostrophe.

Finally, we need the program to do something else if the first statement isn't true. Let's type in the following lines:

```
else :
print 'Hello', name
```

LOOPING AROUND

We can keep this questioning up for ever if we like, which we do by adding a while. It works pretty much in the same way as in Scratch, and we can make it keep going until we stop it. The syntax is this:

```
While <expression>:
<indent> code block
```

```
 ● ● ●          hello.py + (~/Desktop) - VIM
While name! = 'quit':|
~
~
~
~
~
~
~
```

Above: Type in a command so that the loop will continue until you type 'quit' as the name.

We do this by typing in the following:

```
While name!='quit':
```

The exclamation mark (!) means not, as in while name doesn't equal 'quit'. But where should we put this new statement?

If we add it before name=raw_input... an error occurs. If we put it after, it only asks us to type in a name once and then prints that name indefinitely.

To solve this conundrum, we need to give the variable a value – in this case nothing, or to be more precise, an empty string. The program should now look like this:

```
#!/usr/bin/python

name = ' '

while name != 'quit' :
name = raw_input('What is
your name? ')

if name == 'Holly' :
Print 'hi', name, " you're an
awesome individual!"
else :
print 'Hello', name
```

```
 ● ● ●                    hello.py + (~/Desktop) - VIM
while name != 'quit' :
name = raw_input('What is your name? ')
if name == 'Holly' :
Print 'hi', name, " you're an awesome individual!"
else :
print 'Hello', name|
~
~
~
~
~
~
~
```

Above: The complete program.

The code is now indented twice – once for the while loop and once for the if...then statement. You can save this as hello.py and run it by typing in ./hello.py.

OTHER OPTIONS

While Python and Scratch are very popular languages on the Raspberry Pi, they are not the only ways to create programs.

Other options include Java and C++, or even programming at the bare metal level. This section looks at what each approach offers in terms of programming on the Raspberry Pi.

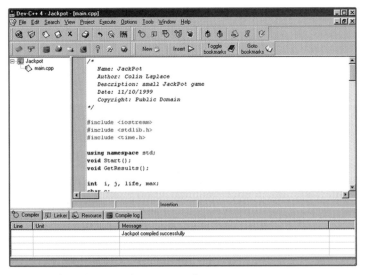

Above: C++ is a popular programming choice.

C++

C++ is a popular mainstream programming language. It is very similar to C in terms of syntax and design, which made the transition for C programmers very easy.

Raspbian includes GCC (Gnu Compiler Collection), which itself includes G++. If for some reason you don't have it, simply fire up a Terminal window and type:

```
apt-get install gcc
```

Most other distributions also feature GCC with C++ support. The best way to check this is to type:

```
g++ -v
```

If G++ isn't installed, enter:

```
sudo apt-get install g++
```

To compile C++ code, you also require the stdc++ header files from the libstdc++ dev package. There is more than one available for Raspbian, because there are four different versions of libstdc++ available.

An integrated developer environment (IDE) called Code::Blocks IDE can be downloaded and installed from the Pi Store website (store.raspberrypi.com/projects/codeblocks).

Your First C++ Programs

Within an IDE or text editor, we can create a simple C++ program. Just type in the following:

```
#include <stdio.h>
int main()
{
    int i;
    for(i=0; i<10; i++)
    {
        puts("Hello,
world!n");
    }
    return 0;
}
```

Save the text as firstprog.cpp and then go to the directory where you saved it and type:

```
g++ firstprog.cpp -o
firstprog
```

This compiles the program into an executable called firstprog. To run the program, type:

```
./firstprog
```

The above example is more like C than C++. The program below has more C++ features.

```
#include <iostream>
int main()
{
    for (int i = 0 ; i < 10 ;
    i++)
    {
        std::cout << "Hello world!"
        << std::endl;
    }
    return 0;
}
```

Above: An example of C++ programming.

JAVA

Java is a programming language and computing platform first released by Sun Microsystems in 1995. It is now owned by Oracle.

Above: Programming in Java.

Programming in Java on the Raspberry Pi requires Oracle Java 8 to be installed. It is a general-purpose computer programming language that is concurrent (actions can happen at the same time, rather than sequentially), class-based, object-oriented and specifically designed to have as few implementation dependencies as possible. This means that programs written in Java can be run on any other platform that supports the language, without needing to be recompiled.

In the early days of the Raspberry Pi, there was a Java development kit (JDK) called OpenJDK. However, this wasn't well optimized for the platform and performance was terrible.

In 2013, Oracle released a JDK specifically for the Raspberry Pi, and the Raspberry Pi Foundation now includes Oracle JDK in its software packages by default.

Developing Java normally requires an integrated development environment (IDE). The problem here is that many Java IDEs do not run well on the Raspberry Pi. However, the release of BlueJ means that you can run an IDE on the Raspberry Pi and write programs using Java SE 8, using standard

Java examples that were previously available on standard computers.

It also allows the creation of interactive objects that represent hardware components connected to the Raspberry Pi, such as LEDs or buttons. This allows for more interactive and experimental set-ups.

Download and Install

1. To download and install BlueJ, open up a web browser on the Raspberry Pi, point it to www.bluej.org, and download the Ubuntu/Debian Linux version of BlueJ.

2. Once downloaded, install the IDE by using the following command:

```
sudo dpkg -i bluej-314.deb
```

3. Then start BlueJ by typing the following:

```
bluej
```

4. When it starts, you can open an existing project or create a new one. Some sample projects are included in the Examples folder under /usr/share/doc/bluej. BlueJ displays a class diagram of the current project in its main window.

Above: BlueJ is an IDE that can be used on the Raspberry Pi.

Above: Download the IDE BlueJ through their website.

You can download some more sample programs from www.bluej.org/objects-first. One such example helps you to create a

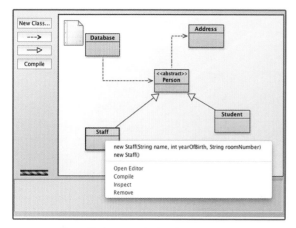

Above: BlueJ programming in action.

program to light up an LED connected to your Raspberry Pi (www.bluej. org/raspberrypi/led.html).

Hot Tip

Some examples of bare metal programming can be found at github. com/dwelch67/raspberrypi.

Above: Programming in bare metal.

BARE METAL

As you might guess from the name, bare metal is programming the Raspberry Pi by directly addressing the device's CPU (central processing unit, or processor) and other components. This means tinkering around with the world of registers, hexadecimal and ARMv6 (or ARMv7) assembly.

Primarily, anyone developing on bare metal is trying to build their own operating system or embedded applications.

The very least you need to get going with programming in bare metal on the Raspberry Pi is to format an SD card and add the files bootcode.bin, loader.bin, start.elf and config.txt. These are the absolute basics of an operating system that can be booted. You also need to place your code in a binary image called kernel.img.

Examples of these files can be found at github.com/raspberrypi/firmware/tree/0671d60180c8d10978b442de5ec9d083596a5f3f/boot.

It pays to know a little about how a Raspberry Pi starts up before running in a bare metal state, or one where an operating system can load up. Bear in mind that this is for advanced users, so the language is very technical.

When the Raspberry Pi is first turned on, the ARM core is off, and the GPU core is on. At this point, the SDRAM is disabled. The GPU executes the first stage bootloader, which is stored in ROM on the SoC. The first stage bootloader reads the SD card, and loads the second stage bootloader (called bootcode.bin) into the L2 cache, and runs it.

Above: The Raspberry Pi starting up.

Bootcode.bin enables SDRAM, and reads the third stage bootloader (called loader.bin) from the SD card into RAM, and runs it. This loader.bin reads the GPU firmware (start.elf). Finally, start.elf reads config.txt, cmdline.txt and kernel.img.

The kernel.img file is where you store code to run an operating system or embedded application.

Unlike most computers, the Raspberry Pi has no conventional BIOS (a set of computer instructions in firmware that control input and output operations). In the Raspberry Pi, various system configuration parameters that would normally be kept and set using the BIOS, are now stored in a text file named config.txt. This is read by the GPU before the ARM core is initialized.

RASPBERRY PI & GADGETS

RASPBERRY PI PROJECTS

The Raspberry Pi can serve you well with just a monitor, keyboard and mouse, but that's only the beginning of its capabilities. Some intuitive individuals have put it to work as the brain in a massive range of devices and contraptions, some of which you'll learn about in this chapter.

CREATE YOUR OWN GADGETS

Most pieces of modern consumer technology have some sort of miniature computer at their heart, from the most powerful games consoles, smartphones and tablets, to coffee machines, garage doors and children's toys. With a Raspberry Pi in your arsenal, you can take a stab at replicating them.

What Can You Do With a Raspberry Pi?

The internet is awash with projects from avid makers who have used the Pi to solve specific issues, such as feeding pets while away from home. Others have used the versatile motherboard to create their very own working mobile phone, just because they can. The science community is using the Raspberry Pi to power new experiments and get to previously unreachable places around the world.

Can I Do It, Too?

Within this aspirational chapter, you'll see eight projects, some more achievable than others. For example, while the wall-climbing robot put together by NASA scientists might be beyond the grasp of beginners, the retro games console is perfectly attainable, because it requires practically no engineering skills. The idea is to show you what can be done and hopefully inspire you to come up with your own ideas.

Skill Requirements

As we mentioned, projects such as the retro games console simply require plug-and-play components and a little software nous. Other projects require additional technology, such as screen components and battery packs, and deep interaction with the Pi's GPIO ports. In some cases, the makers have used advanced techniques such as soldering and breadboarding, both of which are explained in Chapter 7, to achieve their vision. While these pages provide a nice overview of each project, detailed instructions for each (or a more achievable alternative) are available online.

BUILD YOUR OWN MOBILE PHONE

The mobile phone, or smartphone, has become the pre-eminent consumer technology product of our time, surpassing the PC, television and wireless radio before that. But did you know that with a little ingenuity, a Raspberry Pi and a few cheaply obtained components, you can actually build a working mobile handset with relative ease?

DAVID HUNT'S PiPHONE

You've heard of the iPhone, but what about the PiPhone? Professional software engineer and hobbyist inventor David Hunt has managed to create an intriguing steampunk-style handset for around £100/$150. David used the Raspberry Pi and a series of off-the-shelf components (from places such as eBay and component seller Adafruit), enabling the PiPhone to be easily pieced together without the need for an engineering degree.

WHAT'S IN A PiPHONE?

Essentially, the PiPhone pieces together the individual components featured within your everyday mobile phone. The Pi motherboard provides the processing power and memory, while the SIM module, antenna and store-bought SIM card offer the ability to talk to a network. A touchscreen module built especially for the Pi enables data input, while open source software loaded to local storage provides the user interface. A basic lithium polymer battery offers the power source, and audio in/out jacks within the SIM module enable those all-important conversations.

With a few other bits and bobs – including a power converter and a set of hands-free headphones with a microphone boom – and some mild assembly and installation skills,you could be making calls on your Raspberry Pi, too. Here's a list of components from the Adafruit website, which offers an online tutorial.

- Resistive or capacitive 2.8-inch PiTFT touchscreen

- SD memory card, 4 GB or larger

Above: A PiTFT touchscreen.

- ▷ 1,200 mAh lithium polymer battery

- ▷ DC-DC converter

- ▷ FONA and antenna

- ▷ Hands-free headphones with microphone

What Can It Do?

The PiPhone has a fully-capable touchscreen, enabling you to dial numbers and make calls, send text messages and use mobile data, providing there's an active network account (yes, you still have to pay for calls). The PiPhone actually runs off an open source graphical user interface (GUI), a number of which can be downloaded freely from the GitHub platform.

Hot Tip

If you're installing a touchscreen on a Raspberry Pi, you should seek information on calibration. This enables the component to perform as accurately as possible.

Build Your Own PiPhone

The beauty of the PiPhone as a Raspberry Pi-based project is its simplicity. As we mentioned, all the parts are available off the shelf, so you don't even need to get the solder out to make this project a reality. While making it your primary mobile device is probably unfeasible for a variety of reasons (mainly that you can actually buy a fully assembled phone more cheaply), it's a cool project for relative newcomers to cut their teeth on.

Above: David Hunt's PiPhone.

For more information, head over to David Hunt's blog at www.davidhunt.ie, where you'll find a video demonstration and instructions. The Learn.adafruit.com website also offers tutorials and information on assembly, software installation and usage.

The Lapse Pi

Finally, if you're intrigued by the PiPhone, it's also worth checking out David Hunt's Lapse Pi project, which enables the programmable triggering of a camera from a touchscreen-based graphical user interface. The Lapse Pi enables photographers to connect a Pi to their DSLR camera in order to program things such as the number of shots taken and the time delay between each shot. This information as well as details of his other projects is available on his website at www.davidhunt.ie.

Hot Tip

If you're following in the footsteps of Raspberry Pi makers who have shared their creations online, their GitHub pages are an invaluable resource. There you'll find the custom code they've written, and you can install it directly rather than arduously typing in commands step by step.

BUILDING A WILDLIFE CAMERA

The Raspberry Pi is also playing a key role in many conservation projects around the world. The Naturebytes startup has one such project, which aims to 'reconnect people with wildlife through digital making'. The company has built a durable motion-sensing camera, with the Raspberry Pi at its core, combining science, technology, engineering and conservation in one simple package.

THE NATUREBYTES WILDLIFE CAM

This is an exceptionally cool and worthwhile home project, because it enables you to learn about the relatively secret lives of animals that just happen to wander into your back garden. By taking stealthy, high-resolution photos and videos of wildlife, without so much as touching a camera shutter, you can keep tabs on who is sharing your back lawn and also assist with various local conservation efforts.

What is It?

The Wildlife Camera is essentially a
Raspberry Pi, plus the Pi Cam module,
an infrared sensor and a power source
packed inside an attractive and colourful
3D-printed shell. The shell is a clipped
and hinged (it can be padlocked, too)
weather-proof enclosure, which safely
houses the electronics and also
features additional compartments
for the battery pack and other

Opposite, Above and Below: The Naturebytes Wildlife Cam.

modifications. The completed unit looks a little like an attractive bird box, which can stand
freely or be strapped to a tree, for example.

Naturebytes' mission, explained on its Kickstarter project page, is to equip an army of would-
be wildlife watchers with the Wildlife Cam, provide a portal to accept the photographic
submissions, then send the data to active conservation projects.

On its website, the company explains: 'We
could, for example, be looking for hedgehogs
to monitor their decline one month and push
the images you've taken of hedgehogs visiting
your garden directly to wildlife groups on the
ground wanting the cold hard facts as to how
many can be found in certain areas.'

How Does the Wildlife Cam Work?

Like so many of the projects we look at in this
chapter, the Raspberry Pi was chosen because
of its size, versatility and infinite adaptability.

An infrared sensor (PIR sensor), which detects motion within a 12-metre range, is attached to the Pi, which in turn is attached to the Pi Cam module (or the Pi Noir if you're planning to capture nocturnal activity).

If the camera is placed on your bird table, for example, and a bird lands on the table, the custom-made Linux-based operating system instantaneously notifies the Pi, which asks the camera to take a snap. The image or video is saved to the Pi's SD card.

The operation is powered by a large 8,800 mAh lithium polymer battery, which offers 30 hours of uninterrupted tracking. The kit also offers a mini USB charging module, which enables it to run continuously when connected to a power source.

The plan is for users to be able to plug the Wildlife Cam into their television to view the photos (via HDMI) or into their computer (via USB) to transfer and upload them to the Naturebytes website. These photos will then be shared with local conservation projects, which may be tracking the numbers of birds, foxes, hedgehogs, squirrels or any other creatures in a given area.

What Else Can It Do?

The Naturebyes Wildlife Cam kit also makes it easy for you to add other components from the Pi family. For example, you can add a Wi-Fi module to instantly sync the images captured by the camera back to your computer or mobile device. It is also future-proofed for the next generation of hardware and software, enabling users to add wide-angled lenses. There's also a new custom attachment, which enables it to be fitted to more surfaces. Plans are afoot to offer solar panels to keep the battery charged, too.

Can I Build One?

Absolutely! The Wildlife Cam kit can be purchased with or without a Raspberry Pi, and assembly and set-up is simple. It is designed for use in learning environments to enable young users in schools, as well as grown-ups, to assemble, enjoy, code, modify and customize it. The kit includes everything you need to get started. Visit naturebytes.org for more details.

Hot Tip

If adding a Wi-Fi module, you need to ensure that the Wildlife Cam is stationed in a place where it can be picked up by your home router.

BUILDING AN AUTOMATED PET FEEDER

If you're heading out of town, it's not always possible for your four-legged friends to make the trip, too. They need to be fed, but you don't want to just load the bowl and run out on them for a couple of days, do you? You could buy an automated pet feeder, but where's the fun in that? Remember – you now have a Raspberry Pi and a passion for projects.

WHAT IS IT?

David Bryan built a pet-feeding robot that even enables his kitties to have a varied diet when he goes on business trips. The Wi-Fi-enabled model can be remotely operated and vends two different types of food into the food bowl.

How Does It Work?

David bought a regular manual cereal dispenser and replaced the dispensing levers with mechanical servo motors. These now power the turbine that usually releases the tasty treats with a simple twist of the wrist.

He then connected these servo motors to a breadboard (see Chapter 7) in order to make the connections with the GPIO (general purpose input/output) pins on the Raspberry Pi easier and less permanent.

David also used the breadboard to add a human-powered switch (complete with LED lights and a buzzer), for manual operation when the pet owner is at home. This, of course, is completely optional and complicates the project considerably, but is very cool nonetheless.

Once the assembly was complete and the Pi was attached to the motors, David placed the electronics into the hollow dispenser's pillar to

Above: David used a breadboard in his project.

Above: David used a Small-Size Perma-Proto Raspberry Pi Breadboard PCB Kit.

keep everything looking nice and tidy. He also drilled a couple of holes in the pillar to thread through the servo motor wires and USB power cable easily.

With David's freely available code and the installation of a few essential Python programming modules, the Wi-Fi adapter makes it simple to follow programmed release schedules.

David also added some PVC piping to ensure that everything travels neatly into the bowl, resulting in healthy, happy pets who don't miss their owners quite as much.

Hot Tip

Many Pi projects require the soldering of connector cables in order to create secure connections with breadboards. However, you might want to investigate no-solder breakout boards, which offer the chance for less permanent experimentation.

What Else Can It Do?

As with so many of these intuitive and innovative projects, they can be taken much further depending on your imagination and ingenuity. David planned to add a Pi Camera into the mix, in order to track his cat's activity. For your own purposes, this could also be used to ensure the dog isn't eating all the food that's dispensed.

David even wanted to add speakers and sound effects. Those of you old enough to remember *Red Dwarf* will appreciate the Cat character yelling 'Fish!' whenever food is about to be dispensed. He's also planning to build a mobile WebUI to allow everything to be easily controlled from a touchscreen mobile device.

Of course, this device doesn't simply have to be for pet food. If you so desire, you can program it to have your cornflakes ready and waiting for you when you come downstairs in the morning.

Can I Build One?

While this isn't a project you'll be able to do on your own, it is possible with help from an adult. David has kindly posted a list of the kit you need to build a version of his pet feeder. Costs come in at under £100 (about $160) and it can be completed in six hours.

As well as the kit, you need a few tools, too: a soldering iron, drill, some drill bits, a hot glue gun and glue, as well as a wire cutter and pliers. For all the information and a helpful photo gallery, head over to drstrangelove.net.

Above: The completed pet feeder.

BUILD A PI-POWERED CHICKEN MINDER

Chickens seem like low-maintenance, high-reward pets, don't they? Sure, they need to be fed just like a dog, but they don't need walking, won't chew your shoes or pee on your carpet. They even provide you with the most important ingredient in any solid breakfast. However, you need to get up early to let them out and be around at night to ensure foxes don't do what foxes tend to do. One self-confessed 'lazy engineer' concocted a solution with a little help from the Raspberry Pi.

WHAT DOES IT DO?

Chickens aren't like cows – they don't need herding. Just as we retire to our bedrooms at night, so do chickens, so Eric Escobar used the Raspberry Pi to create an automated door for his chicken coop, which rises in the morning when the chickens want to roam wild, and closes and locks at night to keep them safe. His contraption even sends Eric status updates via text message when the door opens, closes or gets stuck.

How Does It Work?

The operation is possible thanks to an independently-powered 12 V DC motor, which anchors a pulley system that both lifts and lowers the door. Because of this, the guillotine-like closing mechanism takes advantage of gravity, so it doesn't squish any chickens on its slow descent to the ground. Once it is closed, the locking mechanism falls into place, preventing any chance of incursion from unwanted predators.

Eric used what are known as Hall Effect magnetized sensors at the top and bottom of the door and its frame. These record when the door is open, closed or stuck. The code Eric has written for the Raspberry Pi forwards a text message to his phone, reading 'Something went wrong, go check the door!' if the sensors don't account for full opening and closing of the door, enabling Eric to rest easy.

Of course, the Pi is hooked up to a Wi-Fi extender, which handles the message delivery from Eric's contraption to his mobile device. It also enables him to program the timings of the opening and closing mechanism, depending on the seasons.

Above: A text is received if the door opens, closes or gets stuck.

What Else Can Be Done?

Don't count your chickens – actually, pretty soon you will be able to count your chickens. Future developments could include the ability to log the chickens' numbers as they come in and out of the coop, so Eric knows that everyone in his flock is accounted for.

Eric envisions predator-deterring gadgets, too. An infrared motion sensor could also be added to raise an alarm if any chickens forget to go to bed or there happen to be predators in the vicinity. All that's missing is an egg collector....

Can I Build One?

Eric has published a complete kit list, electrical diagrams and the installation code for the Raspberry Pi Controlled Chicken Coop Door, making it perfectly replicable. You can find everything on his GitHub page at github.com/ericescobar.

A Remote-Controlled Garage Door

Although more and more people are keeping chickens these days, a more suitable door-related product for suburban folk is this Pi-flavoured solution for a switch-based garage door opener.

Featured on the instructables.com website, it's a much simpler contraption that requires just a few inexpensive bits and pieces beyond the Pi and its power source: a relay, jumper wires and a Wi-Fi adapter, to be precise.

Essentially, the project turns the Raspberry Pi into a web server through a few code modifications and software installations. During this process, a very simple website is uploaded to the server.

When a driver pulls up into the drive, they can load the website on their mobile device and then press a big red button to activate a relay (also wired up to the Pi via the GPIO pins).

Because the Pi acts as a go-between with the physical door switch, activating the relay completes the circuit hooked up to the garage motor and opens the door. It sure beats getting out of the car in the pouring rain.

Visit www.instructables.com/id/Raspberry-Pi-Garage-Door-Opener for everything you need to know.

Hot Tip

Did you know you can use a Raspberry Pi to create a Wi-Fi range extender for your house? See page 163 for details.

A SMART FISHER-PRICE CHATTER TELEPHONE

Before real smartphones came along, with their flashing lights and flying angry birds, the classic Fisher-Price telephone on wheels was all the telephonic fun a toddler could ask for. The toy, which also featured in *Toy Story 3* with a new built-in speaker and speech capabilities, first went on sale in 1962. Over 50 years later, one maker decided to give it a modern twist.

Above: The Smart Fisher-Price Chatter Telephone.

WHAT DOES IT DO?

The recent reissue of the phone enabled young users to physically dial numbers and hear the voices of their favourite *Toy Story 3* characters. Grant Gibson bought the toy for his son, who loved the movie but was decidedly unimpressed with the toy.

Grant decided to add some Pi-based smarts with a little help from a Wi-Fi-based internet connection and some software wizardry.

Now, instead of canned lines from Buzz or Woody, the Chatter Telephone can deliver the latest news, weather and cinema charts, and even offer access to radio stations such as BBC and NPR.

Added Extras

Everything is accessible via a voice-powered menu system by dialling the digits to make selections: 1 for news, 2 for weather, and so on.

There are even push notifications delivered to the phone, thanks to the neat ITTT (If This Then That) platform. This enables Grant to send his family an audio message when he leaves work – a GPS-based geofence recognizes when his phone (and hence its owner) has left the office, and sends out a tweet to a Twitter account. The Twitter account then relays this information to the phone and utters the words 'Woody has escaped from Sunnyside!' As an added bonus, it even plays the Mac OS 9/Wall-E sound on start-up!

How Does It Work?

The engineering required for this project is actually quite limited, according to the inventor. Naturally, the Raspberry Pi replaced the original circuit board, while the original battery box was removed because the Pi provides the power via micro USB. Beyond that, original components have been retained as much as possible.

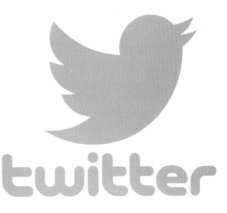

Above: The original battery box was removed as the Pi provides power via micro USB.

Above: Grant added a servo to control eye movements.

The built-in speaker was wired to a 3.5 mm audio jack and hooked up to the Pi's audio-out. The original dial mechanism was soldered to female pin headers, and then connected to the GPIO on the Pi. The mechanical eyes are now powered by a servo motor, rather than the phone's front axle.

The one major upgrade was the replacement of the on-hook sensor with a push-button mechanism, which offered improved reliability.

Indeed, most of the work that went into this weekend project was software-based. Grant wrote a custom script in Python (that he has kindly shared with the community), which enables the Pi to pull in up-to-the minute data from RottenTomatoes.com (for movies) and Forcast.io (for weather reports).

The Pi can also give that information a voice, thanks to the freely available Google Translate text-to-speech tool. Effectively, the Pi calls the service to turn the text into speech, which is then pumped through the speaker.

Above: The phone opened up.

As for the menu options, Grant went to great lengths to employ a voice actor, but there's no reason why individual makers, depending on their needs, can't record tracks themselves.

What Else Can It Do?

What can't it do? This fun project is capable of pulling in data from all sorts of web services. Whether it's sports scores or stock prices, Grant says it's a two-minute job to switch over the APIs and customize the phone for your own preferences. It's also possible to switch out the built-in speaker for an easily affordable and installable speaker for louder volume.

Can I Build It?

If you feel like rehashing your unwanted *Toy Story 3* gadget into a more useful household appliance, you can do so without too much hassle. The code, additional libraries and scripts, plus the parts and mechanical build instructions, can be grabbed from Grant's blog (www.grantgibson.co.uk). Further modification, such as changing the type of information provided when dialling the phone, requires a little more coding skill with Python.

CREATE YOUR OWN RETRO GAMES CONSOLE

Do you ever want to play that old games console? Do you yearn to have one more crack at beating the original Sonic the Hedgehog? Do you pine for an era of playing games that simply involved running and jumping? Well, if you have a Pi, you're in luck.

WHAT DOES IT DO?

This project enables you to play pretty much every significant video game released within a broad 10- to 15-year spectrum (no pun intended). It's a very popular project so there are kits available to shortcut the process (see page 35) and get you up and running even faster! However, with a single Raspberry Pi, a USB controller, some simple plug-and-play computing accessories, and some relatively simple software installs, you can easily recreate a multitude of machines with ease.

Once you've transferred the ROM file (which is a digitized version of the original cartridge or CD), you can easily switch between formats and games.

The Raspberry Pi – especially the newer Pi 3B – offers more power and memory capacity than many of the machines from the early 1990s. The Mega Drive, for example, had 64 KB of RAM, compared to the 1 GB of RAM available on the latest Pi. It has more than enough in the engine room to power these games, including those from the original Sony PlayStation, which is now around 20 years old.

How Does It Work?

This project uses what's known as emulation software, which is able to convince a computer such as the Raspberry Pi to behave as though it is another machine. Many emulators specialize in mimicking one platform, but Emulation Station – which was used for this project – combines them all.

You can load ROM games on to the Pi and play them through the emulator as though you're using the original format. This also enables you to configure a number of affordable USB controllers by associating different buttons with different commands before you begin gaming.

Hot Tip

When downloading ROM files on to your PC, make sure you use anti-virus software to check for viruses and malware before you run them.

The games themselves can be obtained over the internet through emulator websites, downloaded to a PC, and then side loaded on to the Pi via a USB stick or via internet-based file transfer.

Can I Build It?

This project is a largely software-based endeavour, without any of the wiring and soldering required for other DIY projects featured in this chapter, which may come as a relief.

First, you need to install the RetroPie operating system on to the SD card you intend to use (the larger the card, the more games you can fit on it). RetroPie is the best option here, because it has Emulation Station built right in.

Download the disk image on to your PC from PetRockBlock.com and use your favourite PC compression software to unpack it. Prepare the SD card for the Pi by formatting it, then choose a new name for the card. Finally, write RetroPie to the SD card before safely ejecting it from your PC.

Above: The Sega Mega Drive only had 64 KB of RAM; whereas the Raspberry Pi can have up to 1 GB of RAM.

Add the SD card to the Pi (complete with a keyboard, mouse, monitor, Ethernet cable and USB games controller) and then power up. Emulation Station should boot instantly. Before doing anything else, make sure you optimize the available free space on your SD card using the command menu.

Next, configure the controller by navigating through the menu systems in Emulation Station with the mouse and keyboard, and finding Configure Joystick/Controller.

Finally, you need to add your games. There are some ethical issues surrounding this. Piracy is, of course, bad and most emulator websites offer these digitized games to download free of charge. If you can find a way to support the original developer, that's probably the best way to go about it.

We're glossing over some stuff here, but don't worry because there are more detailed instructions for all of this, including links to helpful guides, on websites such as Lifehacker, TechRadar, CNET and HowChoo.com.

What Else Can It Do?

There are lots of ways this project can be enhanced. For example, if you wanted to create a self-contained mini console, you could add a screen, some speakers, a power source and a case, much like the Mini Mac project featured on pages 134–37, only with different software. Adafruit has a cool build-your-own Gameboy kit and project for a totally handheld solution.

If you're unhappy with a wired USB controller, you could add a Bluetooth dongle into the mix.

If you don't mind just plugging your Pi into your TV and the mains power supply, you still might want a nice case to protect your Pi and make it look a little more like a console. There are some neat-looking options on Etsy.

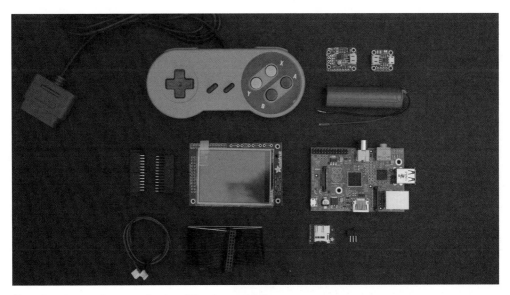

Above: Learn how to make your own Raspberry Pi Gameboy on adafruit.com.

THE WORLD'S SMALLEST MAC

Some Raspberry Pi projects, such as the wildlife camera featured earlier in this chapter, can have a real impact on the world. Others fall into more of a 'because I can' category. The Mini Mac – the world's smallest Macintosh computer – is certainly in the latter camp. John Leake, of the Retro MacCast, built a working one-third-scale version of the original 1984 Macintosh, which fits in the palm of your hand.

WHAT DOES IT DO?

One of the coolest things about the Raspberry Pi – as we've learned throughout this book – is the ability to load it with all manner of software. It can be a blank canvas in that respect. In this case, the inventor used the Mini vMac emulator, which mimics the classic System Software 6 operating system. The software is easily loaded right on top of the Linux-based Raspbian OS.

This enabled John to run all of the original Macintosh software, such as MacPaint, and project it on to a 3.5-inch LCD panel attached to the Raspberry Pi.

Thanks to the Bluetooth adapter inside the Mini Mac, the inventor was able to use a modern wireless Apple keyboard and mouse, too, which the original definitely didn't have. Wired accessories could still be plugged into the back via the available USB and HDMI ports.

How Was It Built?

Once installed, the software boots right from the micro SD card. Easy. But that's only half the story. How did the maker fit all that hardware into the tiny shell and get it all working? First, John had to attach a 3.5-inch TFT monitor to the Pi via the GPIO pins and before attaching it to the front opening of the shell (which he also handcrafted using PVC plastic).

From here, a powered USB hub was attached to the original Raspberry Pi model (this wouldn't necessarily have been needed with the new Pi 3, which has four USB ports), enabling a Bluetooth and Wi-Fi adapter to be connected, as well as an Ethernet adapter, which offers easy access from the rear of the casing. A mains power supply was also squeezed in.

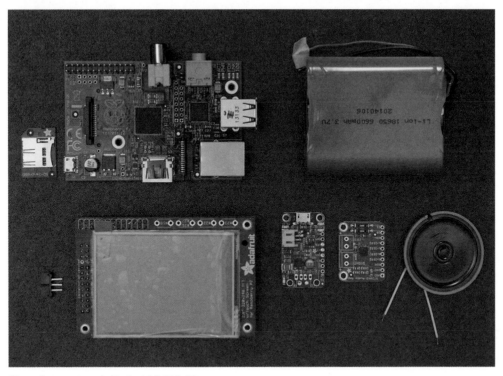

Above: Components needed for the Adafruit Mini Mac.

Above: The Adafruit Mini Mac opened up.

At the rear of the unit are two USB ports for connecting wired accessories, and an HDMI-out for connecting a larger monitor. Sadly, the floppy disk drive opening at the front of the case is just for show.

In order to make everything fit into his scale model, John even had to cut away part of the SD card, but we certainly wouldn't recommend that to beginners.

Can I Build It?

Mac fanatics went wild for John's project, but right now it appears to be one of a kind, which also required serious skill and know-how to build. However, the Adafruit website offers a step-by-step guide for a Mini Mac Pi, inspired by his efforts.

Above: The Adafruit Mini Mac.

Above: The Adafruit Mini Mac.

While it lacks a lot of the original's charm, it is a much simpler construction. Only minor soldering is required, and most parts just fit together very easily.

The Adafruit model originally used a Raspberry Pi Model B, but should also work with the newer Pi 3B. It deploys a 2.8-inch touchscreen, which is easily mounted on to the bezel and attached to the Pi's GPIO using a ribbon cable. It uses a 6,600 mAh lithium-ion battery, which, thanks to a power booster unit (PowerBoost 500C), can last for a full 15 hours. This is all connected to a side switch, which keeps the unit self-contained.

This particular project is also great for those who happen to be interested in 3D printing. If you own a 3D printer, blueprints are available to download. You can also send the plans to an online service that can print and ship the easily assembled casing to you.

Head to learn.adafruit.com/mini-mac-pi and download the PDF for all the details you need.

BUILDING A VOLCANO-CLIMBING ROBOT

The Raspberry Pi might not be the most powerful PC in the world, but for the purpose of a multitude of scientific experiments, it's size that counts. Thanks to its pocket-sized frame, the Pi can boldly go where no PC has ever gone before.

THE STUDY OF VOLCANIC FISSURE VENTS

Geologist and NASA fellow Dr Carolyn Parcheta studies the inside of volcanoes. Now, unless you're Tom Hanks in the 1980s classic *Joe versus the Volcano*, venturing inside an active volcano is inadvisable. Naturally, other avenues need to be explored.

This was a problem to be solved by Dr Parcheta, whose particular area of specialization happens to be the fissure vents from which lava and gases travel to the surface. Because these vents are often extremely deep and narrow, not to mention laced with razor-sharp material, human incursion is a no-no, and as a result very little is known about them. They're also regularly destroyed by eruptions, leaving opportunities for study few and far between.

Meet the Pi-Powered VolcanoBot1

Because of its demure size and endless configurability, Dr Parcheta chose the Raspberry Pi to be the brain of an ingenious wall-climbing robot, which could descend into and scale these constricted corridors with the help of human operators at the surface.

> # Hot Tip
> The internet is teeming with information about incredible Pi projects. The official Raspberry Pi blog (www.raspberrypi.org/blog) lists many of them.

The first VolcanoBot was 30 cm (12 in) long with two 17 cm (6¾ in) wheels. It was tethered to a power supply and a data cable, which enabled it to be lowered into the fissures and still report data back to the surface. During experiments in 2014, the remotely-navigated VolcanoBot reached depths of around 25 metres.

The idea was to use the VolcanoBot to 3D-map the insides of these fissures, in order to gain better understanding of how eruptions occur, so it was fitted with a military-grade infrared reconnaissance camera, capable of seeing in complete darkness. It also boasted Microsoft's powerful open source 3D mapping software Kinect Fusion, helping it to convey information to the scientists at ground level.

In this iteration, the software used shades of yellow to convey distance; the darker the shade, the further away the physical matter was. This data has enabled the geologists to build up complete 3D maps of two of the conduits at Kilauea in Hawaii. There are 54 in total and the work continues.

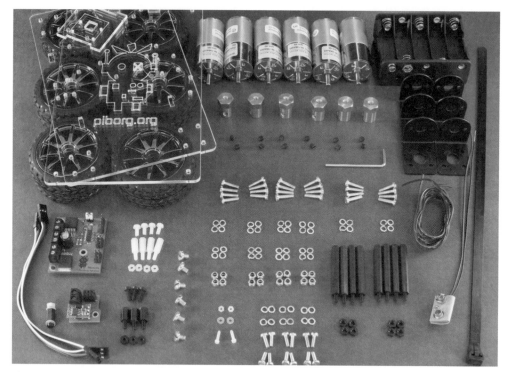

Above: The PiBorg kit for building the DiddyBorg.

Can You Build Your Own?

We're not trying to shatter anyone's dreams here, but replicating highly advanced NASA-grade robotics technology might be a little beyond most folk, ourselves included. We also don't want anyone going anywhere near active volcanoes. Legally speaking, that would be a problem.

However, that doesn't mean there aren't robots that are safe and achievable....

The DiddyBorg

The DiddyBorg, from robotics company PiBorg, is the biggest, strongest and most powerful Raspberry Pi robot on the market. Basically, it's a largely indestructible beast, which you can build.

The battery-powered tank-like vehicle has six wheels and six motors with metal gears. It can climb 45-degree inclines, offers tank steering, supports the Raspberry Pi camera, and can be controlled via Bluetooth by a PlayStation 3 DualShock controller, or by a computer on your network via Wi-Fi. The easy-to-install, open source software also promises automated activity, such as ball following and recon runs.

Build Your Own DiddyBorg

As well as PiBorg, plenty of online specialists, such as ModMiPi, offer everything you need to build your own DiddyBorg. Well, almost everything – you still need a Raspberry Pi (almost all Pis will work), with an SD card and 10 AA batteries, along with any other accessories you wish to add, such as the camera and Bluetooth modules. Tools such as a soldering iron, solder, flat-bladed screwdrivers, wire cutters and an adjustable spanner are also essential, so you will need help from an adult. All of the parts, fittings and screws are included in the kit, which costs £189 (about $244). Detailed build instructions with hi-res photography can be found at www.piborg.org/diddyborg/build.

Above: The PiBorg DiddyBorg.

Above: The PiBorg DiddyBorg.

RASPBERRY PI & THE INTERNET

CONNECTING TO THE INTERNET

Internet connectivity is naturally a huge part of what makes the Raspberry Pi such an effective and versatile piece of technology. With an active web connection, the possibilities are practically limitless. Whether you want to build an internet radio, create a personal cloud server or simply update software, you'll find all you need to know in this chapter.

Whether it's via a good old-fashioned Ethernet cable directly from your router or via the wonders of Wi-Fi, a connection to the internet and the world wide web is essential to get the most from your Raspberry Pi.

CONNECTING TO THE INTERNET VIA ETHERNET

Using an Ethernet cable is definitely the quickest and easiest way to get online with your Raspberry Pi. All you really need to do is run an Ethernet cable (most people have some spares knocking around, but they're cheap enough to pick up) from your web router directly to the dedicated Ethernet port on your Raspberry Pi.

Provided you have an active account with an ISP (an internet service provider such as BT, Sky, Virgin and so on), the network indicator LED lights on the Pi should start to flicker within a couple of seconds and you'll be online. In most cases, no further configuration is required to begin using the web on your Pi. If you have any problems, check out the troubleshooting guide in Chapter 8.

Above: An Ethernet cable is the easiest and quickest method of getting online.

CONNECT TO THE INTERNET VIA WI-FI

If you'd like to go wireless, you need to be using the Pi 3B, Pi Zero W or have purchased a small Wi-Fi dongle for earlier models without Wi-Fi. These dongles can be snapped up quite cheaply. A highly recommended solution is the Edimax EW-7811Un, which supports internet speeds of 150 Mbps, has good range and does not require a separate power source. Visit www.elinux.org/RPi_USB_Wi-Fi_Adapters for a list of dongles that are currently supported. Adding Wi-Fi takes a little longer to set up, but doing so using the GUI (graphical user interface) is very straightforward.

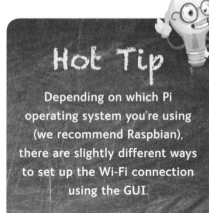

Hot Tip

Depending on which Pi operating system you're using (we recommend Raspbian), there are slightly different ways to set up the Wi-Fi connection using the GUI.

Connect Via Wi-Fi Using the GUI

The easiest way to hook up to a Wi-Fi connection is to use the graphical user interface within your chosen OS for the Raspberry Pi. If using Raspbian, for example, an icon should show up in the toolbar or the desktop when the device is plugged in.

Click this to choose from the available networks within the pop-up menu. Next you need to type in the network key (usually printed on the router somewhere). Once connected, the signal strength shows on the network icon within the toolbar.

Setting Up Wi-Fi Using the Command Line

1. Open a terminal window and type:

```
sudo nano /etc/wpa_supplicant/wpa_supplicant.conf
```

2. Go to the bottom of the file and add the following:

```
network={
    ssid="Your_ESSID"
    psk="Your_wifi_password"
```

3. If you are using wpa_passphrase you can use:

```
wpa_passphrase "Your_ESSID" "Your_wifi_password" >> /etc/
wpa_supplicant/wpa_supplicant.conf.
```

Note that this requires you to change to root (by executing sudo su), or you can use the following without changing to root:

```
wpa_passphrase "Your_ESSID" "Your_wifi_password" | sudo tee
-a /etc/wpa_supplicant/wpa_supplicant.conf > /dev/null
```

4. Now save the file by pressing Ctrl+X, then Y, then finally press Enter.

5. At this point, `wpa-supplicant` will normally notice a change has occurred within a few seconds, and it will try and connect to the network. If it does not, restart the interface with `sudo wpa_cli reconfigure`.

6. Check if the connection is successful by using `ifconfig wlan0`. If the 'inet addr' field has an address beside it, the Raspberry Pi has connected to the network.

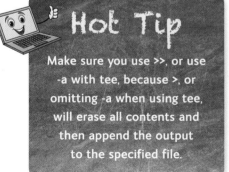

Hot Tip

Make sure you use >>, or use -a with tee, because >, or omitting -a when using tee, will erase all contents and then append the output to the specified file.

Advantages of Wi-Fi

Of course, the main advantage of connecting wirelessly is the improved portability of the Raspberry Pi. Without long wires, the Pi can be as far away from the router as the range of the router takes it. This is great for some of the projects mentioned in the previous chapter, which require the Pi to be outdoors.

Hot Tip

If you're having trouble connecting through Wi-Fi, ensure the Broadcast SSID setting is enabled within the router's console.

Disadvantages of Wi-Fi

While this makes the Pi much more portable, using Wi-Fi will soak up more power, and too many Wi-Fi networks in a small area can be confusing, so best turn it off if you definitely aren't using it. Also, Wi-Fi service isn't always as stable as a wired connection, so using Ethernet for testing or troubleshooting is often a good idea to rule out Wi-Fi issues.

FINDING AND MANAGING YOUR IP ADDRESS

Once you've taken the steps to set up the Ethernet or Wi-Fi connection, you should have an active Internet Protocol (IP) address. Here's all you need to know about IP address discovery and management.

WHY DO YOU NEED TO FIND YOUR IP ADDRESS?

Any device that is connected to a local area network has an assigned IP address. Finding your Pi's IP address is an important step in confirming your connection to the internet, but it also has plenty of other uses, which we'll go into during this chapter.

Find Your IP Address Using the GUI

Just as it was with connecting to the internet, finding your IP address is much easier when using the graphical user interface. If you connected via Wi-Fi, all you need to do is click the Wi-Fi configuration icon on the desktop. The familiar pattern for an assigned IP address is 192.168.x.x.

Find Your IP Address with the Terminal

Again, open the Terminal of your Raspberry Pi and type sudo ifconfig. Depending on the nature of your connection, your IP address is listed in the etho (Ethernet) or wlan0 (Wi-Fi) sections of the text that appears on screen.

Above: If using the graphical user interface, double click the Wi-Fi configuration icon.

Hot Tip

Your Pi is just as useful without a keyboard, mouse and monitor of its own. You can access the Pi by connecting it to another computer, either remotely or using physical cables.

```
                              pi@raspberrypi: ~                          _ □ ×
File  Edit  Tabs  Help
pi@raspberrypi ~ $ sudo ifconfig
eth0      Link encap:Ethernet  HWaddr b8:27:eb:d5:f4:8f
          UP BROADCAST MULTICAST  MTU:1500  Metric:1
          RX packets:0 errors:0 dropped:0 overruns:0 frame:0
          TX packets:0 errors:0 dropped:0 overruns:0 carrier:0
          collisions:0 txqueuelen:1000
          RX bytes:0 (0.0 B)  TX bytes:0 (0.0 B)

lo        Link encap:Local Loopback
          inet addr:127.0.0.1  Mask:255.0.0.0
          UP LOOPBACK RUNNING  MTU:16436  Metric:1
          RX packets:0 errors:0 dropped:0 overruns:0 frame:0
          TX packets:0 errors:0 dropped:0 overruns:0 carrier:0
          collisions:0 txqueuelen:0
          RX bytes:0 (0.0 B)  TX bytes:0 (0.0 B)

wlan0     Link encap:Ethernet  HWaddr 00:0f:53:a0:04:57
          inet addr:192.168.1.10  Bcast:192.168.255.255  Mask:255.255.0.0
          UP BROADCAST RUNNING MULTICAST  MTU:1500  Metric:1
          RX packets:136 errors:0 dropped:0 overruns:0 frame:0
          TX packets:52 errors:0 dropped:0 overruns:0 carrier:0
          collisions:0 txqueuelen:1000
          RX bytes:11995 (11.7 KiB)  TX bytes:6016 (5.8 KiB)

pi@raspberrypi ~ $ ☐
```

Above: Here you can see the IP address 192.168.1.10 next to the wlan0 entry.

Finding the IP Address without a Monitor or Keyboard

If you have speakers or headphones connected to the audio-out (perhaps if you're using it as a media streamer), reboot the device and the IP address is read out on reboot. This is a particularly handy trick if you don't have a keyboard or monitor connected to the Pi.

Giving the Raspberry Pi a Static IP Address

As we mentioned, the IP address is automatically assigned to the Pi when connected to a router via Wi-Fi or Ethernet. This is called dynamic IP, which means it can change all the time. A static IP address helps if you wish to access the Pi remotely, because you'll know the address is always the same.

There are many guides to performing this online, but ModMyPi.com offers a great way to ensure your Pi's IP address always stays the same. Here's a guide based around those instructions.

Create a Static IP Address

1. Open the Terminal, type `sudo ifconfig` and check you are connected to the internet.

2. You need to take down some notes about the current connection and router. Write down the following information with a paper and pen.

    inet addr – 192.168.1.81 (Pi's current IP address)

    Bcast – 192.168.1.255 (Broadcast IP range)

    Mask – 255.255.255.0 (Subnet Mask Address)

3. Before we can proceed, we need a little more information, so type the command:

```
netstat -nr
```

    This should give you a little more information to jot down. Record the information next to Gateway Address and Destination Address.

Above: If your Raspberry Pi is not connected to a keyboard, reboot to find out the IP address.

4. Now we can finally set about modifying the network settings using all of the information we've collected. To edit the network configuration, we need to deploy the Nano text editor again, so type `sudo nano /etc/network/interfaces` into the command line.

5. Find the section that reads `iface etho inet dhcp` and change it to `iface etho inet static`.

6. You need to manually add all of the address information we gathered in the previous steps. Type in the headers and add the values you collected. The address field will be the static IP always associated with the Pi once the process is complete.

```
address
netmask
network
broadcast
gateway
```

Hot Tip

Having a static IP address is essential when using the Pi to build a personal cloud storage server. See page 171 for a guide.

7. Once this stage is completed, you can exit Nano by hitting Ctrl and X, and hitting Y to save the changes. You need to check it all worked, so first clear any existing data by entering this into the Terminal:

```
sudo rm /var/lib/dhcp/*
```

8. Next you can reboot your Pi using the command `sudo reboot`. Upon restart you can check your new settings by typing `ifconfig` into the Terminal. To check everything is working, ping the Gateway address by issuing the following command: `ping *enter address here* -c 10`

TESTING AND USING THE INTERNET

Now you're all connected, be it to a wired or wireless network, you'll want to take that connection for a spin. In the previous section, we explained how to find IP addresses and ping routers to confirm the connection. However, there's only one sure-fire way to ensure everything is working correctly. Let's do a little cyber loafing.

THE EPIPHANY WEB BROWSER

The Raspbian operating system – which the vast majority of people will be running on their Pi – ships with the Epiphany web browser (as of September 2014), a sleek and lightweight program perfect for perusing the world wide web from your Raspberry Pi.

A big improvement on the original default browser Midori, Epiphany enables you to enjoy the internet just as you would on your PC, to a certain extent. You can even watch YouTube and Vimeo videos in high definition.

Opening and Using Epiphany

The web browser will be familiar to anyone who has used traditional browsers, such

Above: The Epiphany browser.

as Internet Explorer, Firefox and Google Chrome. There's the address bar, the forward and back buttons, and the search field, as well as an interface that enables you to skip between multiple tabs.

How to Start Browsing the Web

1. Click the Epiphany icon (the globe logo with a cursor) on the desktop or find it in the programs menu. This loads the home page.

Above: The Epiphany icon.

2. Click within the address bar and type in the URL for the website you wish to visit. Hit Enter and the web page loads within the window.

3. If you wish to search the web instead, you can type your query within the Search box to the right of the address bar.

Step 1: The Epiphany browser can be found via the programs menu.

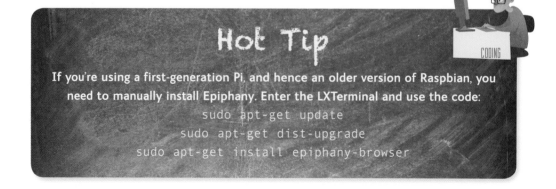

Hot Tip

If you're using a first-generation Pi, and hence an older version of Raspbian, you need to manually install Epiphany. Enter the LXTerminal and use the code:

```
sudo apt-get update
sudo apt-get dist-upgrade
sudo apt-get install epiphany-browser
```

Above: You can still watch YouTube videos at high definition.

Advantages of Epiphany

Epiphany (aka GNOME Web) may be
lightweight and clutter-free, but it still packs
the latest web technologies. It can handle
larger JavaScript-heavy websites, enable faster
web scrolling, play 720p YouTube videos
and easily stream music from the web. Even
playing some graphics-heavy web-based
games isn't a problem.

Hot Tip

In order to watch YouTube, you
need to tell the site to use the
HTML5 player rather than Flash.
Browse to www.youtube.com/html5
in Epiphany.

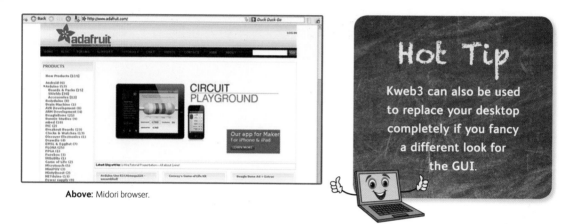

Above: Midori browser.

> ## Hot Tip
>
> Kweb3 can also be used to replace your desktop completely if you fancy a different look for the GUI.

Other Web Browsing Options

Just like the array of operating systems (or distros) you can store on your Raspberry Pi, there's also plenty of alternative web browsers if you'd like to try something other than Epiphany. Installing other browsers is just a case of opening the LXTerminal and punching in simple commands.

- **Midori:** The first default browser within the Raspbian OS lacks the pace and modernity of the Epiphany browser, but remains well used.

- **Chromium:** If you have a Raspberry Pi 2 or original Raspberry Pi B, you can install the Chromium browser, which is a stripped-back open source version of the Google Chrome browser you may be used to using on desktop or mobile devices. To install it, open Terminal and punch in `sudo apt-get install chromium-browser`

- **Kweb3:** Another web browser built exclusively for the Raspberry Pi is Kweb3. It's easy to install, has support for HTML5, full A/V support and the ability to natively open PDF files. Installation instructions change with the version number, so head here for the simple command line instructions: www.raspberrypi.org/forums/viewtopic.php?t=40860

MAKING A WI-FI HOTSPOT WITH THE RASPBERRY PI

There are far more interesting things you can be doing with a Raspberry Pi, but if you need a new Wi-Fi router (modem) or need to create a wireless access point (AP), your pocket-sized PC can do that, too. It can also be useful for creating a separate Wi-Fi network in your house for guests to use.

WHAT YOU NEED TO CREATE A WI-FI HOTSPOT

In terms of hardware, these projects are quite simple because there's no breadboarding, soldering or any of that malarkey involved. Many Pi users will also have everything they need at their disposal.

All you need is an active Raspberry Pi, a power supply, an SD card with the Raspbian OS installed, an Ethernet cable, and either a Wi-Fi-enabled Pi or a Wi-Fi adapter plugged into the USB socket of the Pi. If you're going to use it around the house, a case for the Pi comes in handy just to keep it safe from bumps. Let's also assume that you're connecting to the Pi with your own mouse, keyboard and monitor.

Hot Tip

An absolute must here is the need for the Wi-Fi adapter (if you have a separate one) to support Access Point mode. Check before you buy or attempt this project.

Above: Need a new Wi-Fi router? Use your Raspberry Pi to create a Wi-Fi hotspot instead.

Installing and Configuring

Once you've got the gear together and everything is up and running as normal, it's down to the software installations and some command configurations to bring this project to life. For many of the projects in this book, we've offered directions to online instructions, but for this example, we'll provide the full list of instructions.

There's a lot to go through in the command lines, but with a little patience, you'll be up and running in no time. There are several helpful guides online, but we'll talk you through the main steps here (we tip our hat to www.elinux.org/RPI-Wireless-Hotspot).

Pre-Steps

1. Update your Raspbian installation:

```
sudo apt-get update
sudo apt-get dist-upgrade
```

2. Install all the required software in one go with this command: `sudo apt-get install dnsmasq hostapd`

3. Since the configuration files are not ready yet, turn the new software off:
```
sudo systemctl stop dnsmasq
sudo systemctl stop hostapd
```

Configuring a Static IP

We are configuring a standalone network, so the Pi needs to have a static IP address assigned to the wireless port. We're assuming that standard 192.168.x.x IP addresses will be used on our wireless network, so we will assign the server the IP address 192.168.0.1. It is also assumed that the wireless device being used is `wlan0`.

1. First, the standard interface handling for wlan0
    needs to be disabled. Type: `sudo nano /
    etc/dhcpcd.conf`.

2. Add `deny interfaces wlan0` to the end
    of the file and save the file.

3. Then add: `sudo nano /etc/network/
    interfaces`

4. Find the `wlan0` section and edit it so that it
    looks like the following:

```
allow-hotplug wlan0
iface wlan0 inet static
    address 192.168.0.1
    netmask 255.255.255.0
    network 192.168.0.0
```

5. Now restart the dhcpcd daemon and set up the new `wlan0` configuration:

```
sudo service dhcpcd restart
sudo ifdown wlan0
sudo ifup wlan0
```

Configuring the DHCP Server (DNSMASQ)

The DHCP service is provided by dnsmasq, and by default, the configuration file contains a lot
of information that is not needed, and it is easier to start from scratch.

1. Rename this configuration file, and edit a new one:

```
sudo mv /etc/dnsmasq.conf /etc/dnsmasq.conf.orig
sudo nano /etc/dnsmasq.conf
```

2. Type this information into the dnsmasq configuration file and save it:

```
interface=wlan0  # Use the require wireless interface - usually
wlan0
dhcp-range=192.168.0.2,192.168.0.20,255.255.255.0,24h
```

Installing the Software and Creating a Wi-Fi Router

1. Edit the hostapd configuration file, located at /etc/hostapd/hostapd.conf, to add the various parameters for your wireless network: `sudo nano /etc/hostapd/hostapd.conf`

2. Add the information below to the configuration file. This configuration assumes we are using channel 7.

```
interface=wlan0
driver=nl80211
ssid=NameOfNetwork
hw_mode=g
channel=7
wmm_enabled=0
macaddr_acl=0
auth_algs=1
ignore_broadcast_ssid=0
wpa=2
wpa_passphrase=Password
wpa_key_mgmt=WPA-PSK
```

```
wpa_pairwise=TKIP
rsn_pairwise=CCMP
```

3. We now need to tell the system where to find this configuration file. Type:
```
sudo nano /etc/default/hostapd
```

4. Replace the line #DAEMON_CONF with:

```
DAEMON_CONF="/etc/hostapd/hostapd.conf"
```

5. Then start everything back up:

```
sudo service hostapd start
sudo service dnsmasq start
```

6. Congratulations! Your Pi is now acting as access point; there's just one more step to creating a full wireless access point, and that is to create a bridge between the Pi's Ethernet port and the wireless network you're just created. Type:

```
sudo apt-get install hostapd bridge-utils
```

7. Since the configuration files are not ready yet, turn the new software off:

```
sudo systemctl stop hostapdnable
```

8. Then type: `sudo nano /etc/dhcpcd.conf`, and add `denyinterfaces wlan0` and denyinterfaces eth0 to the end of the file and save.

9. Add a new bridge, which in this case is called br0. Type: `sudo brctl addbr br0`

10. Connect the network ports. In this example, connect `eth0` to `wlan0`. Type: `sudo brctl addif br0 eth0 wlan0`

11. Now edit the interfaces file to adjust the various devices to work with bridging:

```
sudo nano /etc/network/interfaces
allow-hotplug wlan0
iface wlan0 inet manual
```

12. Add the bridging information at the end of the file.

```
# Bridge setup
auto br0
iface br0 inet dhcp
bridge_ports eth0 wlan0
```

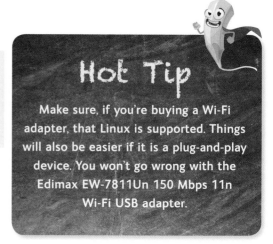

Hot Tip

Make sure, if you're buying a Wi-Fi adapter, that Linux is supported. Things will also be easier if it is a plug-and-play device. You won't go wrong with the Edimax EW-7811Un 150 Mbps 11n Wi-Fi USB adapter.

13. Follow the process to set up the hostapd.conf file, but add `bridge=br0` below the `interface=wlan0` line, and remove the driver line.

14. Now reboot the Pi.

Connecting Devices to Your New Wi-Fi Network

Now your home Wi-Fi network is up and running, and the Pi routes any traffic to your wired router through the Ethernet cable. In order to connect your devices, such as a laptop, smartphone or tablet, you can find your new network listed in the Wi-Fi section of the settings. It's under the name you gave it earlier. Enter the password and you're good to go.

Setting Up Remotely

There's more than one way to skin a cat, as the old adage goes, and the same is true for this project. If you're using the Pi as a headless machine (meaning you don't have a keyboard, monitor and mouse connected), you can perform the commands on a Windows computer, using an SSH platform called Putty (instructions here:

Above: Edimax EW-7811Un Wi-Fi adapter.

www.raspberrypi.org/documentation/remote-access/ssh/windows.md). Or you can plug a console cable into the Pi's GPIO to access the Terminal (learn.adafruit.com/adafruits-raspberry-pi-lesson-5-using-a-console-cable/overview).

USING THE PI TO EXTEND YOUR INTERNET CONNECTION

Of course, most people these days have a wireless connection in their homes and offices, but the signal doesn't always stretch all the way across the house, let alone out into the garden. Walls, doors and floors make sure of that.

Luckily, in just the same way that this project enables wired networks to become wireless, it can also be used to extend the range of a wireless network. All you need is to use a longer Ethernet cable from your router to the Pi set-up described above. Place it strategically and you should have uninterrupted Wi-Fi throughout the house and even outside, too.

Hot Tip

Pi projects that require the device to be outdoors, such as the Wildlife Cam mentioned in Chapter 4, benefit from the extension of the Wi-Fi network. Of course, this means owning multiple Pis, but an avid maker can never have enough.

BUILD AN INTERNET RADIO PLAYER

Turning a Pi into a device capable of streaming radio stations from the internet has become a popular hobby among makers. This project requires piecing together some simple engineering, programming and even a little 3D printing, but soon enough you'll be rocking out to BBC 6 Music or relaxing with Radio 2.

WHAT DOES IT DO?

The web has plenty of innovative ways to create an internet radio player from the Raspberry Pi (check this out for example: amrhein.eu/Radio2). However, there are simpler ways to do it, as evidenced by George Kouloris and Arthur Schmitt (pseudonym tart2000) and their Raspdio project. They placed the Pi inside an attractive 3D printed case and added a button and a volume dial for simple controls. There's a small speaker connected, too, keeping everything in a neat package.

HOW IT WORKS

Once pieced together, Raspdio makes it possible to pick up a web-based stream of a radio station of your choice. To achieve this, the Pi uses software called the Music Player Daemon (MPD) and its front-end client, the Music Player Client (MPC). This pairing underpins most internet radio projects, including the one on page 168, which adds a touchscreen to the mix.

As well as having an on/off switch, the Raspdio uses a Google spreadsheet to effectively turn it into a radio alarm clock.

Above: George Kouloris and Arthur Schmitt's internet radio.

Check out the Instructables page featuring the Raspdio for the lowdown on the project: www.instructables.com/id/Raspdio

Above: A Google spreadsheet can be used to make the Raspdio function as a radio alarm clock.

WHAT YOU NEED

This project requires some software installation skills, as well as a little engineering nous. If you don't have a 3D printer (and let's face it, few of us do), the plans are available to download as STL files, so the attractive case can be made through a third-party company and shipped to you.

You need a Raspberry Pi up and running on Wi-Fi and a mini 3.5 mm speaker to get things going. However, you also need a push button to act as the on/off switch, a potentiometer, a sweet-

Above: You'll need a push button to act as the on/off switch.

looking knob to act as the volume control, and an ADC (analogue-to-digital converter), so the digital Raspberry Pi can read the analogue output signals.

Finally, you need a breadboard in order to hook these analogue components up to the Pi's GPIO pins.

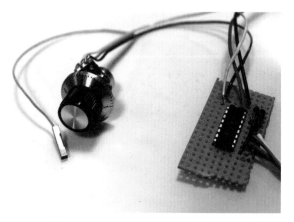

Above: The potentiometer (volume control) needs to be attached via an ADC.

How to Build It

This is by no means an easy build, but the creator has been kind enough to offer detailed step-by-step hardware and software instructions. The first step is to hook the speaker up to the Pi via the 3.5 mm jack. The Pi is also kind enough to provide the speaker with the power it needs through the 5 V GPIO pin. This is the easiest bit!

Next, the button needs to be connected to the GPIO pins to enable the radio to be turned

Hot Tip

Want something more advanced? There are plenty of internet radios out there with LCD screens and added buttons, making it easy to switch between stations.

on and off. Finally, the volume rocker is created when the potentiometer and the ACD are combined along with a breadboard (*see* Chapter 7 for a guide to breadboarding) to connect to the Pi itself.

From here, it's software-based. Your Wi-Fi-enabled Pi is equipped with a host of tools, including the URL for an internet radio stream and a Google spreadsheet, which tells the Raspdio when to begin auto-playing and when to switch off.

The code is available for all of these tasks on the maker's GitHub page, and it can be edited for personal preference.

Once everything is installed, the product can be assembled within its 3D case and – hey presto! – you've built an automated internet radio that, if you wish, can wake you every morning, or ease you off to sleep with your favourite station.

Can I Build It?

Because there are some components you may not have encountered before, as well as some more challenging means of assembly, this may not be a project you can jump into straight away, but it's certainly achievable with a little learning on the fly. We think the coolness factor makes it worth the effort alone.

Above: Hooking up the speaker.

BUILD AN INTERNET RADIO WITH A TOUCHSCREEN

As if being able to access radio stations on your Raspberry Pi wasn't enough, one keen maker added a touchscreen and designed his own user interface, making it easy to control the music in his freestanding internet streaming device.

WHAT DOES IT DO?

This project follows on from what was achieved in the previous section. It provides online access to a host of great music playback via your Raspberry Pi's internet connection and some speakers. However, whereas the previous version offered some buttons and a simple LED display, this one gets a little touchy-feely.

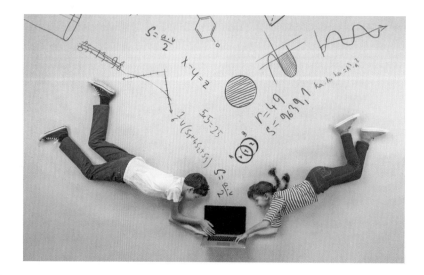

Spencer Organ's project added touchscreen controls via a custom-designed interface he has made available to download over the internet. His Radioplayer program makes it easy to switch stations, adjust volume, play/pause and identify tracks with a tap of the screen.

Above: The user interface makes it easy to play/pause and change the station or volume.

The project also runs from a portable power supply and is pieced together and enclosed in a way that makes it one of the most attractive, self-contained Pi projects out there.

What You Need

As well as your Pi, with an SD card running Raspbian OS and an internet connection (Wi-Fi or Ethernet), you also require the following:

- **A PiTFT 320 x 240 2.8-inch touchscreen display**: Preferably pre-assembled, because this will not require any soldering and can just be plugged into the Pi.

- **A power supply**: A micro USB battery or mains adapter.

- **A Raspberry Pi case**: From somewhere such as Adafruit, in order to keep everything safe and tidy.

How to Build It

The first step is to connect the Raspberry Pi to the touchscreen display. However, it is not just a plug-and-play solution. Software must be installed to make it play nicely with the Pi and run the GUI and the Terminal. Calibration

with a special program also boosts the performance of the touchscreen and enables it to be operated more accurately. Performing these steps gave Spencer a portable Pi without the need for a keyboard, mouse or monitor.

Once everything is up and running, he installed the open source MPD (Music Player Daemon), which plays audio files, organizes playlists and maintains a music database. This is a background tool, so

Above: Getting the PiTFT touchscreen working.

the front-end MPC (Music Player Client) software was also installed. Once this was complete, Spencer used the Pi's console to add access to the internet streams for his favourite stations in order to create a playlist.

In terms of managing the stations once installed, Spencer created Radioplayer in Python, the Pi's main programming language. This is the touchscreen interface that controls MPC Radio and makes it easy to switch between stations, adjust volume and more.

There's also an indicator to tell you whether you're online/offline, while there's a bar to show the name of the station and the track that's being played.

Can I Build It?

This project requires no engineering nous and the maker has provided detailed instructions to replicate the project, as well as making his custom software available to download. So with some basic knowledge, this is definitely one of the more replicable projects out there. Apart from the touchscreen and the case, there is very little additional financial expenditure required. Go to: learn.adafruit.com/raspberry-pi-radio-player-with-touchscreen/installing-the-radioplayer for the full guide.

CREATE A PERSONAL CLOUD SERVER

There are loads of solutions for keeping all your documents online and accessible wherever you go. So-called cloud solutions such as Dropbox and OneDrive are very popular. However, there are ongoing privacy concerns with these services, and acquiring lots of storage space is not cheap. But did you know that you can use the Raspberry Pi to build your very own cloud?

WHAT DOES IT DO?

The cloud is big business these days, with many people switching from local file storage on hard drives to online platforms. These solutions make digital files available on multiple devices, while keeping them safe from hardware failure and loss. Dave Bennett's project enables users to build their very own cloud storage area using the Pi and an external hard drive.

In this instance, the Raspberry Pi is deployed as an always-on always-connected Linux-based computer. The advantages to this are that it is small, lightweight and can run around the clock without using much power and costing a fortune in electricity. Because you're providing your own hard drive, there are no additional storage space costs either. This also means you don't have to trust big corporations such as Apple, Google or Microsoft with your files. The result is easy access to your important files from devices on your or other networks.

Above: Create your own cloud server with an external hard drive connected to the Pi's USB port.

What You Need

This is a very low expense project, designed to save you money. Dropbox, for example, costs £7.99 ($10) a month for one terabyte of storage, or £79 ($100) a year.

- **A 1 TB external USB hard drive:** This can be plugged into the Raspberry Pi and costs less than £50 ($80), meaning you're already up on the deal.

- **A functioning Raspberry Pi:** You need the Raspian OS installed and an active internet connection, along with a power supply to keep the Pi running at all times.

Above: Using the Pi to build a cloud server can be cheaper than using Dropbox.

Hot Tip

The Instructables.com website has created a custom disk image for this project that enables you to skip the majority of the steps listed in this section. It does most of the coding work for you and saves you tons of time.

- **An account with the OwnCloud platform:** Once you've installed the functionality on your Pi, you can log in at OwnCloud.com and access any files saved to the Pi on any device.

How to Build a Personal Cloud Server

This project is the brainchild of popular YouTube channel host Dave Bennett, whose helpful guides have over 100,000 subscribers. Listen to this dude – he knows what he's talking about.

First of all, the Pi needs to be configured and connected to the internet. Then the Pi must be assigned a static IP address, which we covered earlier in this chapter (see page 150). Once this process is complete, the Pi has to be rebooted (you know `sudo reboot` by now, right?).

Above: Build a box to contain and protect your Pi-made cloud server.

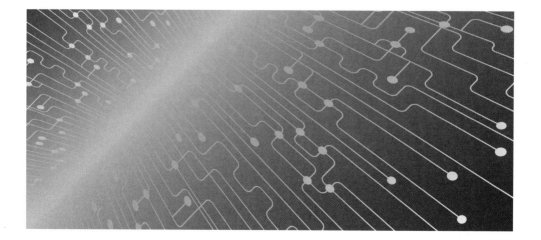

Above: Access OwnCloud and create your own login.

The next step, as always on the Pi, is to update the software packages to ensure you have the very latest tools available. This is done by typing `sudo apt-get update` in the Raspberry Pi Terminal.

Next Dave installed a whole pile of stuff on the Pi to enable his mission, a list of which can be found listed on his website (www.davebennett.tv/create-your-own-personal-cloud-server).

Then there are a few more finicky Terminal-based tweaks, such as setting up a PHP accelerator to speed things along, setting a maximum file upload size for the drive, and setting up an SSL certificate.

Above: Start uploading your files.

The next step is to install and set up the OwnCloud platform on the Raspberry Pi, before connecting the hard drive to the Pi's USB port and mounting it in order for the storage locker to play nicely with the device.

Next, access OwnCloud by entering the IP address of the Raspberry Pi (see page 149 for finding IP addresses) in a web browser. This enables you to create your own login. Using a client for Windows, Mac, Linux or whatever, you can start uploading all your files to OwnCloud and they're sent straight to the hard drive you've set up via the Pi.

Can I Build It?

Yes! You absolutely can. The assembly of this project from a hardware point of view could not be simpler. Meanwhile, there are detailed written and video instructions available from a number of online sources (www. instructables.com/id/Raspberry-Pi-Owncloud-dropbox-clone for example). If you're happy to have a Pi constantly running and wish to avoid the mainstream cloud services, building your own cloud server is definitely an attainable goal.

TECH SPECS

As well as being a great internet device, a perfect programming tool for novices, and a vessel for all manner of exciting robotics projects, the Raspberry Pi is a wonderful piece of kit for audio and video.

The Raspberry Pi has everything you need to store, stream and play your favourite media content. Whether it's streaming audio from the internet and playing it through Wi-Fi speakers, or sending stored videos to your connected display, the Pi can handle it with ease.

HOW TO CONNECT YOUR PI FOR A/V CONTENT

Thankfully, there are plentiful options when connecting a display to your Pi in order to enjoy video content – and more often than not, you'll have at least one of these options around the house.

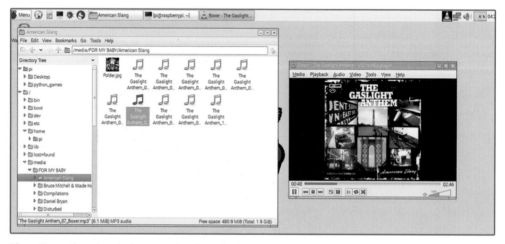

Above: You can play audio and video content through your Raspberry Pi.

HDMI Out

In much the same way as you'd hook up a Blu-ray player or set-top box, HDMI from a Pi to a monitor carries high definition pictures (1080p resolution) and audio to the display and built-in speakers. As such, this is the best way to enjoy the highest quality video.

Hot Tip

If you have an old DVI monitor, you can hook it up via an HDMI-to-DVI adapter. However, in this instance you won't be able to view video content at HD resolution.

Composite Video Out (Only on Model A)

On the original Raspberry Pi Model A, there's a yellow port for a composite video cable. This enables you to connect an older analogue TV or monitor to the Pi via a composite video cable (or SCART).

3.5 mm Audio Jack (Model A)

For Raspberry Pi Model A users, the 3.5 mm jack enables you to connect the Pi up to headphones or a stereo. However, it also provides the sound connection to your monitor when using the composite video.

Composite A/V Out (Model B, Pi 2 and Pi 3)

On newer versions of the Pi (Model B and Pi 2), the composite video out has been combined with the audio out for a space-saving all-in-one A/V solution. This versatile out means you

Hot Tip

If you want to use your Pi to record sound, you can plug in a USB microphone.

Above: Newer versions of the Pi have a combined audio/visual out.

can still plug headphones and power speakers into the 3.5 mm out, but you can also plug in a 3.5 mm A/V cable for stereo audio. The red and white cables provide sound, and the yellow cable provides the video. The Pi Zero has composite out capabilities, but these require soldering.

Above: Wi-Fi adapter.

Bluetooth and Wi-Fi

While you can't connect displays to the Pi wirelessly, you can use Wi-Fi or Bluetooth adapters to stream audio to compatible speakers over short ranges (*see* page 183).

WHAT CAN THE PI PLAY?

While the Pi has all the tech know-how to play audio and video files, it does not support all video and audio formats, of which there are dozens. In this section, we're focusing on playing audio. *See* page 192 later in the chapter for information about playing video.

Supported Audio Formats

As with video, there's a smaller range of audio files that are supported out of the box. MP3 is supported, for example, as are plenty of file extensions such as M4A and FLAC.

Configuring Audio Output

While the Pi is programmed to play audio content from the default source, you can easily change from HDMI to headphone jack (or vice versa) in the command line.

1. Enter the Terminal and issue the following command: `amixer cset numid=3 2`

2. This lists the sources. HDMI is 2 and the headphone jack is 1. For automatic detection of the audio source, enter 0.

3. This can also be performed using the Configuration screen. Enter sudo raspi-config into the command line to bring up the interface. Then hit Advanced Options (option 8), and select option A9 to change the audio output.

Step 3: Press option 8 to bring up the Advanced Options in the Configuration screen.

How to Play an MP3 File Using the Command Line

Providing you have MP3s loaded on to your SD card or an external hard drive, you can play them through the command line. This is done via Omxplayer, Raspbian's built-in video player.

1. Open the LXTerminal and type in cd (change directory) to browse to the place where you have audio stored on your Pi. For example: cd /home/pi/

2. Issue the command omxplayer example.mp3 (replacing example with the actual name of the file).

3. Provided the Pi is plugged into headphones or a monitor with speakers, you should now hear the sound. You can press X to exit.

Install a Test Audio File

To quickly test an audio file (*see* the example above), you can visit a site such as www.freespecialeffects.co.uk. Find the audio sample of your choice, then issue the following command in the LXTerminal to download it:

```
wget http://www.freespecialeffects.co.uk/soundfx/household/
filename1.mp3
```

Then you can repeat the steps listed in the previous section to play it.

Above: You can browse your audio files through the GUI (graphical user interface).

Copying Audio Files on to Your Pi

You're probably wondering how to get all of this nice audio on to your Pi. Probably the easiest way is to copy all of the files you want to play on to the same SD card. The larger the card, the more tunes you can fit on it. From there, you can browse to them through the GUI (graphical user interface) or via Omxplayer, as discussed above.

Using a Media Centre to Play AV Content

Using the command line and Omxplayer is the least user-friendly way to play an audio or video file. Thankfully, there are simpler solutions, which we cover in this chapter, such as the Kodi media centre and the Pi Music Box, both of which enable you to access an entire world of content without messing too much with the Terminal side of things.

STREAMING AUDIO WITH YOUR RASPBERRY PI

In the previous section, we learned how to play a simple MP3 file on the Raspberry Pi, but if you're connected to the web, there's a whole world of audio goodness just waiting to be streamed.

WHAT CAN I STREAM ON MY RASPBERRY PI?

While it's possible to play your own digital music collection by plugging a USB stick into a Pi, streaming music is the way forward. Through some minor hardware and software configuration, you can stream audio from the web and even music you have stored on your networked devices.

Getting Started with Audio Streaming

In order to begin streaming audio, it helps to install some server software. The likes of the Music Player Daemon (MPD) and Media Player Classic (MPC) are great tools to have. One you see and one you don't.

MPD sits in the background and does all the hard work. When you tell it to play a stream, the software will chase it down and convert it to an audio output. MPC is the client you deal with in the Terminal, and it gets all the credit.

Using MPD and MPC to Stream Internet Radio

Installing this pairing offers a simple proof of concept when it comes to streaming audio from the internet. Here's how to install the package and configure your Pi to play an internet radio station.

1. Installing the software is as simple as opening Terminal and typing `sudo apt-get install mpd mpc`

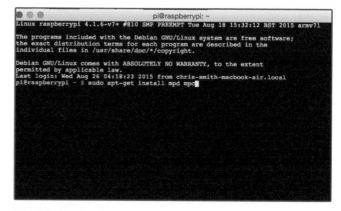

2. This is more of a check than a change, but to ensure the permissions are correct, issue the following commands:

Step 1: Installing the software is easy. Open the Terminal and type this.

```
sudo service mpd stop
sudo chmod -R g+w /var/lib/mpd
sudo chmod -R g+w /var/run/mpd
```

3. Make a quick change to this directory: `sudo nano /etc/mpd.conf` Where the file says `bind_to_address  "localhost"` change it to `# bind_to_address  "localhost"`

4. Now you can reboot your Pi using the command `sudo shutdown now -r`

5. Upon the reboot, you can add a live radio stream in order to get started. Type the command `mpc add` followed by a live stream address (for example, `mpc add http://www.radiofeeds.co.uk/bbc6music.pls` adds BBC 6 Music).

6. Type `mpc play` and hit Enter to begin playing.

7. Typing `mpc help` shows a host more tools you can use in the Terminal, such as `mpc stop`

8. Use the `mpc add <insert stream url>` command to add more stations (a web search will help you find the URLs) to your playlist. You can switch between them by using `mp3 prev or mpc next`

Step 6: The live radio stream will now start playing.

Hey presto! You have an internet radio loaded with all your favourite stations.

Streaming Audio in GUI Using VLC

If you prefer working in the GUI (provided you have a connected monitor), you can stream live radio or any internet-based web stream using the VideoLan Player (VLC), which is a popular program you may have encountered for Mac or PC.

1. You can install VLC on your Pi by opening the Terminal and typing: `sudo apt-get vlc`

Step 1: You can install VLC through typing this in the Terminal.

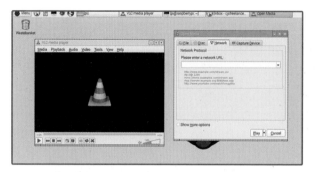

Step 3: You can copy and paste a URL directly into the program.

2. Once the package has installed, you can open VLC. This enables you to open streams via the web browser in VLC.

3. If you find a stream address (URL), you can copy it directly into the program by going to Media then Open Network Stream in VLC. Copy and paste the URL and hit Enter.

Improving Sound Quality

A few sacrifices were made when putting together the Raspberry Pi. One was incompatibility with some audio formats (meaning not everything you find will play), and another was lower-grade audio hardware. As a result, the audio output isn't of the best quality.

For those who care about how their audio sounds, a plug-and-play USB sound card (such as the Daffodil US01) is a good addition to any streaming set-up. For the best results, get a board such as the HiFiBerry, which plugs directly into the GPIO pins.

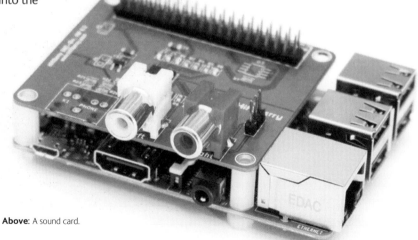

Above: A sound card.

NETWORK STREAMING PROJECTS

You can install one simple disk image on your Raspberry Pi, hook it up to your stereo and access live internet radio, a world of podcasts, a massive library of tracks from your favourite artists and even songs stored on other devices. There are multiple projects we could have included here, but why bother with installing numerous solutions when just one can do it all?

THE PI MUSICBOX

Pi MusicBox is aptly described as the Swiss Army knife of streaming music via the Raspberry Pi. You can connect to Spotify or Google Music streaming services, listen to your favourite podcasts from iTunes, and also access live radio stations from around the world using TuneIn Radio. It was developed by Wouter van Wijk, and is based on the Modipy server tool.

What You'll Need

You'll need a Raspberry Pi (obviously!) plus a means of connecting to your stereo unit, either via the HDMI out or the 3.5 mm jack (or perhaps via an amplifier if your speakers don't have one). You'll need an SD card loaded with the MusicBox software, and a wired

Hot Tip

If you're serious about your sound, get yourself a sound card to plug into the Pi. It'll improve the quality no end.

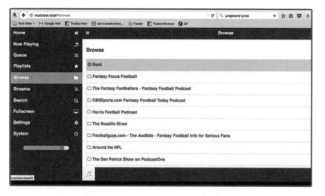

Above: Transfer the MusicBox install file from your SD card to your Pi and install.

Above: Open a browser and type in musicbox.local.

connection to an internet network, plus, of course, the internet. Once set-up is complete, you can go wireless with ease. If the pi MusicBox is going to be a permanent feature in your stereo unit, you might want to get a nice case, too.

Download the Pi MusicBox Operating System

Use your computer to download and unzip the install file from www. pimusicbox.com. Then you need to write the .IMG file to your SD card using your favourite tool. Once the process is complete, you can transfer it to your Pi and boot up to install.

Using MusicBox in a Web Browser

Once the Pi is up and running, you can leave it alone – everything is now controlled via the web interface on your other devices. Ensure your Pi and your secondary device are connected to the same internet network, open a web browser and type `musicbox.local` into the address bar.

Above: The Browse option in MusicBox.

What you'll see is a full interface, enabling you to play tunes through a host of different sources. It's touch-friendly, so it works on keyboards or mobile touchscreens.

Listening to Music

There are three main ways to access music using the MusicBox:

Above: Paste in the desired URL of the stream and hit Play. You can also save the stream with a name for easy access later on.

- **Browse**: This offers options to search within the various services, such as iTunes Podcasts, Spotify and TuneIn. You can move through categories in order to find your selection.

- **Streams**: This section is perfect if you know the URL for the radio station, podcast, YouTube link or Spotify playlist you want to listen to. Just copy it into the field and press Play. You can also give it a name and save it to the list for easy access. For example, to listen to Radio 5, you can copy in http://www.radiofeeds.co.uk/bbc5live.pls and hit Play. If you wish to autoplay that particular URL when the Pi boots, you can go to Settings, then MusicBox, and copy that URL into the Autoplay section. Save the changes and reboot the Pi.

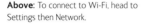

Above: To connect to Wi-Fi, head to Settings then Network.

Step 2: Switch AirPlay on.

Hot Tip

If you have a USB drive full of music, you can plug this in and access all of those artists, albums and tracks under the Local Tracks heading in the Browse section.

- **Search:** If you're looking for something in particular – such as a band's library from Spotify, a radio station via TuneIn or a podcast from iTunes – you can search here and start playing.

Connecting to Wi-Fi

Once everything is configured, you don't have to worry about trailing an Ethernet cable from your router – you can easily set up Wi-Fi access. In the musicbox.local web page, head to Settings then Network, and enter the Network ID and Password.

Bonus for iPhone and iPad Users

If playing music from an Apple mobile device, such as an iPhone or iPod, you can enable the AirPlay technology. This means you can send audio from any app to the Pi, rather than using the musicbox.local website. Spotify, Apple Music, BBC iPlayer, you name it, it can be sent to the Pi.

1. In musicbox.local on your Apple device's web browser, open Settings and select MusicBox.

2. Scroll down to AirPlay and switch the slider to On.

3. Begin playing music on your Apple device through any app, ensuring you're connected to the same network as your Pi.

4. Swipe up from the foot of the screen to access the command centre and select AirPlay.

Hot Tip

Android users can also stream from their devices using the DNLA settings in MusicBox. It can be enabled in Settings and must be paired with a DNLA streaming app for Android devices.

5. You should see MusicBox as an option. Select it and enjoy the music coming through your speakers via the Pi.

PLAYING VIDEOS USING THE RASPBERRY PI

As well as a powerful tool for playing all manner of audio files, the Raspberry Pi can also be used as a great video playback device. You can load your favourite digital movies on to the Pi and also access them from the internet.

ATTACHING A MONITOR

In the early part of this chapter, we discussed the ways to hook the Pi up to a monitor. While you can operate the Pi as a headless machine in order to play audio, obviously you'll need a screen in order to view videos.

Supported Video Formats

The default Raspberry Pi video player is Omxplayer, and it can play most video files encoded with the H.264 video codec. Providing that's the case, the Pi can play popular digital video files with extensions such as .AVI, .MOV, .MKV, .MP4 or .M4V. It even plays some .FLV (flash video) files if they're encoded with the H.264 codec. It'll be a case of trial and error. You'll find some files work and others don't.

Buying New Video Codecs

You can also purchase additional codecs, such as the MPEG-2 format, very inexpensively from the Raspberry Pi store to open up more file types (www.raspberrypi.com/mpeg-2-license-key).

Working with Incompatible Video Files

If you're really desperate to play a certain video file on your Pi (perhaps if it's for the video looper project described later in this chapter), you can re-encode it using a PC or Mac.

A popular, free program such as HandBrake enables you to encode in the H.264 codec. You can then feed it back to the Pi and you'll be good to go.

Playing Video Via the Command Line

As we learned in the audio section, you can play media through the command line, via Omxplayer, as long as the file is stored in a directory on your Raspberry Pi. To play a video file stored on your Pi's desktop, for example, do the following:

Above: A free program like HandBrake can convert a video to H.264, so it can then be played on your Pi.

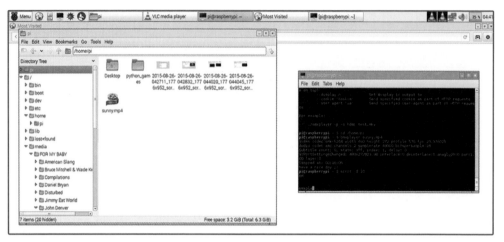

Above: Playing a video with Omxplayer through the command line.

1. Issue the command `cd /home/pi/Desktop` to switch to the directory where the video is stored.

2. In order to play, you need to open Omxplayer, followed by the name of the video file, and hit Enter (for example, `omxplayer sunny.mp4`).

3. The video should begin to play. You can hit Space to pause it, or X to exit.

Useful Omxplayer Commands

You can type `omxplayer help` at any time to bring these up, but here are some commands you may find useful when controlling video (and indeed audio) using the keyboard.

- **Space**: Pause/resume
- **Up arrow**: Jump forward 30 seconds
- **Down arrow**: Jump back 30 seconds
- **i**: Previous chapter
- **o**: Next chapter
- **+**: Increase volume
- **-**: Decrease volume
- **q**: Exit Omxplayer

Hot Tip

If you're getting video but no sound, make sure the audio is coming from the HDMI. Issue the command omxplayer -o hdmi example. mp4 when loading a file.

You can do all of this without entering the point-and-click world of the GUI, and you'll probably feel like a computing badass while doing it, too. Alternatively, *see* below.

Watching Video in the GUI

As you have a monitor connected, there's no real need to mess around in the command line. If you have files on your SD card or a USB drive, you can watch them directly in the GUI. You can browse

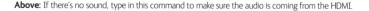

```
● ● ●                          pi@raspberrypi: ~
Linux raspberrypi 4.1.6-v7+ #810 SMP PREEMPT Tue Aug 18 15:32:12 BST 2015 armv7l

The programs included with the Debian GNU/Linux system are free software;
the exact distribution terms for each program are described in the
individual files in /usr/share/doc/*/copyright.

Debian GNU/Linux comes with ABSOLUTELY NO WARRANTY, to the extent
permitted by applicable law.
Last login: Wed Aug 26 05:14:20 2015 from chris-smith-macbook-air.local
pi@raspberrypi - $ omxplayer -o hdmi sunny.mp4
Video codec omx-h264 width 480 height 272 profile 578 fps 23.976025
Audio codec aac channels 2 samplerate 48000 bitspersample 16
Subtitle count: 0, state: off, index: 1, delay: 0
V:PortSettingsChanged: 480x272@23.98 interlace:0 deinterlace:0 anaglyph:0 par:1.0
0 layer:0
```

Above: If there's no sound, type in this command to make sure the audio is coming from the HDMI.

through the file folders and double-click on files to begin playing them in Omxplayer. You can also make use of the same keyboard commands explained above, too.

VLC

Although VLC is great for audio, trying to play videos when using the Raspbian operating system will lead only to frustration as the two tools do not play nicely with each other. There are easier options for playing video, such as OSMC, as explained later in this chapter.

MAKING A PI SPY SURVEILLANCE CAMERA

The Raspberry Pi's camera module opens up a whole new world of possibilities for makers and hobbyists. In this case, you can set up a spy camera in your home and view the live stream from any device.

WHY BUILD THE PI SPY?

Home security cameras, such as those made by Nest, are great, but they are expensive. They're also quite conspicuous. With a Raspberry Pi at your disposal, you can cheaply build your own solution, access the content from outside the home, and find a good hiding place around the house where only the camera module pokes out.

Above: Raspberry Pi camera module.

What You'll Need

This is another relatively simple project for the Raspberry Pi, with minimal additional hardware needed in order to make it work. Naturally, you need a Raspberry Pi camera module. The only other extra hardware you need is a power supply. In terms of software, you will need to install some free, open source software known as MotionPie.

Installing MotionPie

MotionPie is a custom open source operating system, which can be easily installed on to the Raspberry Pi. On the front end, it enables you to log in and view all of your footage in real time, and at the back end it handles all of the video footage captured by the Pi.

It's easy to install, thanks to the makers at MotionPie, who have wrapped it up as a custom boot image for the Pi and other single-board computers. All you need to do is browse to their GitHub page using your Mac or Windows computer (github. com/ccrisan/motionpie) to download the latest version.

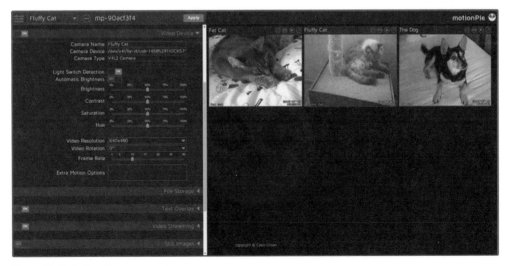

Above: The MotionPie software.

Once you've downloaded the file, use your favourite unzipping tool and burn it to a fresh SD card (*see* page 59). Now you can safely eject the card and insert it into your powered-off Raspberry Pi.

How to Build and Configure the Pi Spy

Before we power up, we need to assemble our surveillance camera.

1. Insert an Ethernet cable and the camera module, as instructed on page 145.

2. Power up the Pi and be patient, because the first boot takes a while.

3. Find your Pi's IP address using the instructions laid out on page 149, or use an iOS or Android app called Fing to discover devices on your Wi-Fi network. Look for the device under the line 'Raspberry Pi Foundation' to find the IP address.

4. Make a note of the IP address and then enter it into a web browser on a secondary device. You're now on a MotionPie website, and if you've performed the above steps correctly, you'll see what your Pi camera sees.

Step 3: You can use the Fing mobile app.

Securing the Camera and Setting Up Wi-Fi

There are a couple more steps that need to be taken in order to secure the camera and keep other eyes away.

1. On the MotionPie website, click on the key graphic, which brings up a box asking for a username and password.

2. Type admin and leave the password field blank.

3. Next click the Admin menu and select Advanced Settings. This enables you to set up your own username and password.

4. Finally, set up the Wi-Fi on your Raspberry Pi by switching the Wireless Network slider to On. Then type in your Network ID (SSID) and password, and hit Save. Now you can disconnect the Ethernet cable from the Pi.

Deploying the Pi Surveillance Camera

Now the set-up is complete, you can type the Pi's IP address into the web browser on any device of your choosing, and see a live video feed from the device. All you need to do now is find a good place to hide it!

The Next Steps

While this is a super cool project to test out the capabilities of the Pi camera module, there are plenty more directions you can go, thanks to MotionPie. For example, it can also record video to the SD card or a USB drive. It's also capable of time-lapse recording, meaning you can watch a few hours of action in a matter of minutes. It has a motion-sensing mode, too, so it starts recording when it detects movement.

Above: Watch a live video feed from your Pi surveillance camera.

HOW TO MAKE A VIDEO LOOPER

The Raspberry Pi can simplify the process for anyone who wishes to have video content playing on a loop on any screen. No hooking up laptops, no burning DVDs.

WHY CREATE A RASPBERRY PI VIDEO LOOPER?

If you go into many businesses or attend art exhibitions, you often see digital signs running promotional video content on a loop. In the past, this has usually been achieved by burning a DVD and running it on repeat, or by plugging a laptop into a screen and doing likewise. The Raspberry Pi offers a more streamlined solution, and a video loop is very easy to set up. The advantage here is that the Pi is very small and can be hidden away neatly behind the monitor.

Above: The Raspberry Pi eliminates the need to burn DVDs in order to play looped video content.

Hot Tip

The Omxplayer is a good option for Pi video projects because it's optimized to use hardware acceleration, meaning it uses the Pi's graphics processing unit for more efficient playback of high-resolution video files.

What Can it Do?

This project features a customized version of the operating system, which interfaces with the default Omxplayer, in order to pick up videos from a USB stick and play them (in order, if there's more than one) in a constant loop. Videos can be played in full HD 1080p (depending on your monitor) with audio support.

What You'll Need

Beyond an internet-connected Raspberry Pi (Wi-Fi is preferable because it's more portable) and a power supply, all you really need here is a compatible display and a USB drive containing the videos you wish to play, in a file recognized by the computer.

Installing the Software

This is one of the easiest projects you'll find in this book, and the kind folk at Adafruit have provided a complete guide and all the software you need to install (learn. adafruit.com/raspberry-pi-video-looper/ overview). As with many projects, you need to start with a fresh install of the Raspbian OS on an SD card (see page 58).

Then, either via the Pi itself or through a remote SSH connection (see page 163), simply install the custom-built looper:

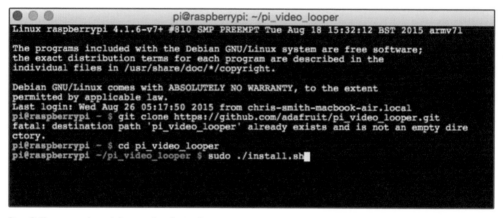

```
pi@raspberrypi: ~/pi_video_looper
Linux raspberrypi 4.1.6-v7+ #810 SMP PREEMPT Tue Aug 18 15:32:12 BST 2015 armv71

The programs included with the Debian GNU/Linux system are free software;
the exact distribution terms for each program are described in the
individual files in /usr/share/doc/*/copyright.

Debian GNU/Linux comes with ABSOLUTELY NO WARRANTY, to the extent
permitted by applicable law.
Last login: Wed Aug 26 05:17:50 2015 from chris-smith-macbook-air.local
pi@raspberrypi ~ $ git clone https://github.com/adafruit/pi_video_looper.git
fatal: destination path 'pi_video_looper' already exists and is not an empty dire
ctory.
pi@raspberrypi ~ $ cd pi_video_looper
pi@raspberrypi ~/pi_video_looper $ sudo ./install.sh
```

Step 2: The commands needed to complete the installation.

1. Type: `git clone https://github.com/adafruit/pi_video_looper.git`

2. Hit Enter and then copy in the following to complete the installation:
    ```
    cd pi_video_looper
    sudo ./install.sh
    ```

3. Hit Enter again and within five minutes the installation should be complete.

If the install was successful, you'll see the message: 'Insert USB drive with compatible movies' on your connected screen.

Insert USB drive with compatible movies.

Step 3: If you see this message, the software was successful installed.

Above: After inserting the USB, a message will display the number of movies detected, and start a countdown.

Adding and Playing the Videos

In order to get the videos looping via the Pi, you need to add them to a freshly-formatted USB stick. Transfer the video files to the stick using a secondary computer in the same way you usually do, and eject it safely. Plug the stick into the Pi.

Playing the Video Files

Once the Pi detects the USB stick, the display should inform you how many videos have been discovered. There's a 10-second countdown and then the video playback begins. If there's more than one clip, the gap between videos is only about 100 milliseconds. If you have speakers on your TV or monitor, you hear the audio, too. Videos continue to play until you remove the drive.

Customizations

Although the default set-up works tremendously well, there are customization options, too. So, for example, you could run the videos from the SD card rather than a USB stick, or change the default video player from Omx. For full details, check the Adafruit page at learn.adafruit.com/raspberry-pi-video-looper/overview.

MIN   MAX

VOLUME

TURN YOUR RASPBERRY PI INTO A MEDIA CENTRE

While playing audio files through the command line is fun, it's not exactly efficient. With the attractive and versatile Open Source Media Center (OSMC) software, you can harness the power of the Kodi media player in your Pi's GUI.

What Can it Do?

Once you've downloaded OSMC (Kodi) on to your Pi, you can access a wide range of media content; whether it's locally-stored audio, video or photos, or similar content from the web. It's great if you don't have a modern Smart TV and wish to have internet capabilities, too.

Above: The My OSMC menu page, which lets you control your settings.

Downloading Kodi on to an SD Card

The best way to obtain this software is to use a Windows or Mac computer to download and install Open Source Media Center on a new SD card (not one you're using for other activities). This creates a bootable image you can then run on the Raspberry Pi.

1. In your web browser, head to OSMC. tv and then select Download from the home screen.

2. Choose Raspberry Pi from the list of supported devices.

3. Select Windows/Mac/Linux to indicate the computer you're currently using.

4. Click Here to start the download and installation process. Then you need to run the file and it begins to download.

5. Once the download is complete, a set-up box appears for OSMC. You need to follow some on-screen instructions to install it.

6. Select your language and the device you're using (Pi 1, 2 and so on), and hit Next.

Above: With Open Source Media Center you can access a wide range of content.

Step 2: On the download screen, select Raspberry Pi from the list of devices.

Step 5: Follow the on-screen instructions to install OSMC.

7. Then select a version of the software you want to install and where you'd like to save the program (SD card, USB stick and so on).

8. Next you need to prepare how you want OSMC to connect to the web. If you choose Wireless, you need to input your network information.

9. Choose the drive to install on and accept the licence. This installs the software.

Hot Tip

You can control OSMC through the various peripherals connected to a Pi, either wired or wirelessly via Bluetooth. However, if you have an IR adapter, you can also configure other remote controls to access your media.

10. Once this process is complete, you can add the SD card to the Pi and boot up. OSMC should boot up directly in a new GUI, following a brief install process. Your Pi then reboots before loading the interface.

Installing Channels and Plug-ins

Of course, when you first install OSMC, you'll have nothing to play. You can fix this by adding video and audio add-ons to access content over your web connection. For example:

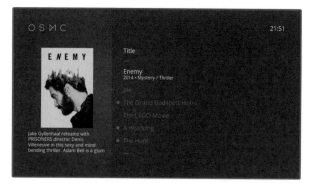

Above: Playing a video in OSMC player.

1. Browse the menus to Video.

2. Select Video Add-ons from the menu.

3. Pick a channel (YouTube, for example) and install.

4. Open the channel and use prompts such as search, popular or channels to find and play content.

Playing Your Own Media Content

In order to play content you may have saved to an external hard drive or a USB stick, you need to plug that into the device, too. OSMC should instantly recognize the drive. Here's how to access the content on the drive.

1. Browse to Audio and select Files from the menu.

2. The name of the drive should appear in the list. Select it.

3. Clicking the file should instantly load the video, providing it's a file the Pi is compatible with (see page 193 on formats). This works for video files and photos housed on your storage device of choice.

Change the Appearance of the OSMC

The default interface is a little dry and involves lots of sorting through lists. Thankfully, there are options to change what's known as the skin of the media player.

1. Browse to Settings then Appearance.

2. From the Skin menu, pick Confluence for a more dynamic UI.

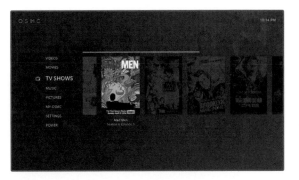

Above: You can change the appearance of the interface to make it look more dynamic.

OSMC and Kodi (XBMC)

You may have heard a lot about the XBMC/Kodi media player when it comes to the Raspberry Pi. Essentially, we're talking about the same thing. OSMC is the software that brings the Kodi (formerly known as XBMC) software to life and makes it compatible for use on the Raspberry Pi in a bootable image.

HOW TO MAKE A VIDEO CAPTURE UNIT

As well as playing video content, the Pi is also capable of capturing and storing footage. With the help of a camera module and some additional hardware, one maker put together a fully functional automated video camera for use at home or on the go.

WHY MAKE A VIDEO CAPTURE UNIT?

There are several great uses for such a project. With the aid of a mount or tripod, it could easily act as a dashboard camera when driving, a home surveillance camera, or a wildlife camera to keep an eye on the creatures sharing your back garden.

Above: Xxxxxxxx

What Can It Do?

Once assembled, the video capture unit is able to record footage on a loop. This means that once the memory card is full, it begins recording from the beginning again, overwriting the old footage. This unit automatically starts recording on boot up and can be simply halted by safely powering down the machine. With a continuous power supply, it can run and run, continuing to record on a loop, replacing old uneventful footage with new stuff.

Above: Video capture unit.

The footage is also transferrable and can be viewed on a PC by easily removing the USB drive used to store it. While the footage is captured by the camera's default H.264 video format, it can easily be converted to MPEG4 for easier management.

Can I Build It?

The machine, put together by Matt Hawkins at the Raspberrypi-Spy website, isn't the easiest project in this book, but it was designed to be replicable. There is a little building skill required so you will need help from an older friend or parent, but all of the software code is provided.

Matt chose to place his unit within a standard case with drilled holes for the LED lights, a simple on/off switch and a camera lens. The LEDs and switches were connected up to the Pi's GPIO switches via a BerryClip (an add-on board used to easily connect new components). Some assembly is required here (see Chapter 7).

Power was provided to the Pi via a USB charging solution, which enabled the unit to be used on the go, away from the mains for a considerable period. Here's a rundown of what else was used to make this project:

- A Raspberry Pi (Model B).

- A simple, affordable Cyntech case for the Raspberry Pi.

- An 8 GB SanDisk SD card with a fresh Raspbian install.

- A 32 GB Kingston Flash Drive to store the video footage.

Above: Cyntech case.

- A camera module to capture the footage, connected to the CSI port (*see* page 39).

- An 8 mm metal washer for the outside of the casing to attach a magnetic lens.

- A (3D printed) tripod mount, attached to the Pi case. You can attach a regular mount, but it won't look as pretty.

- A RAVPower RP-PB13 14,000 mAh USB power bank to offer mobile power.

A simpler, bare-boned set-up is detailed on the Raspberrypi-Spy website.

How to Set Up the Software

The hardware line-up depends on your preferences, budget and skill level, but to replicate the functionality, there are certain things you have to do on the software side.

Above: RAVPower USB power bank.

Thankfully, Matt provided his custom code for his project and made it available to download online. This includes the configuration settings, the means of starting the program on boot, and the ability to define how many video files are kept and the duration for which they're kept.

> ## Hot Tip
>
> If you'd prefer to save the files to the SD card, rather than a USB stick, this is possible, but transferring files to a PC isn't as simple.

Once powered up, it's important to update the Pi with the latest software (*see* Chapter 1) and to configure the connected Pi camera module (*see* page 198).

At this stage, Matt's custom code can be downloaded and installed, and a USB drive can be mounted in order to ensure video files are written to the card.

Can I Build It?

This is a beginner-to-intermediate level project. If you choose to replicate it fully, you need some moderate assembly skills, but the project can be adapted to suit your own needs and budget. Full instructions for software assembly can be found at www.raspberrypi-spy.co.uk.

Above: The project can be adapted to your needs, such as adding a tripod to the capture unit.

GOING FURTHER

GETTING A CASE

It's well worth getting a case to protect your Raspberry Pi. There are lots of different ones available, so choosing the right case can be quite tricky. You can either purchase a case or make one yourself from scratch. However, you should make sure you get the right kind of case to fit your device – for more detail about the different kinds of Pi, *see* 'Two Iterations of the Device' on page 22.

WHAT DOES A CASE NEED?

You should buy a case that is sturdy and gives you access to all the ports, both ribbon spaces and the general input/outputs, so you have the option to add attachments later. Some cases suit certain projects better than others. You should also consider ventilation, so the Pi doesn't overheat.

Where Can You Buy Cases?

Cases can be purchased online from:

- eBay.co.uk
- Amazon.co.uk
- RaspberryPi.org
- Adafruit.com

They're also available on the high street from these retailers:

- CEX
- PC World/Currys

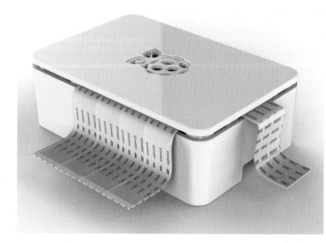

Above: A OneNineDesign case.

What Cases Can You Buy?

- **Official Raspberry Pi case**: This case is very affordable, at around £6 ($10), and has good access to the ports.

- **Pibow Coupé Model 2, B+**: This case gives good access to all the GPIOs and top components, and will cost you around £8.50 ($12).

Above: The official Raspberry Pi case.

- **UniPi case**: This all-aluminium case has great ventilation and enables you to stack multiple Pis that have the same case, although it's quite expensive at around £32 ($50).

What Kind of Case Can You Make?

- **A DIY Lego Pi case**: Try using Lego to build your perfect Pi case. You can include doors to cover access ports, and customize it as your projects develop.

Above: The Pibow Coupé case.

- **3D printed Pi case**: Check the Pi's dimensions, search for 'Pi case designs' online, then order through Shapeways. com or Sculpteo.com.

- **Punnet cardboard case**: You can download the free PDF for this case from RaspberryPi.org. Print out and build.

Above: A Lego case made by Richard Hayler.

OVERCLOCKING

Overclocking changes the limits on your Pi's components. Overclocking earlier Pis was popular, especially for gaming, but the newer chipsets are made to tighter tolerances, so there is less need for overclocking generally.

WHY OVERCLOCK YOUR PI?

Some overclock settings are considered 'supported' by the Raspberry Pi Foundation, but it may shorten the lifespan of your Pi. There are some settings that flip a hardware switch inside the Pi and void the warranty, these are: over_voltage greater than 6; force_turbo=1; and temp_limit greater than 85.

How to Overclock Your Pi

Here's how to go about boosting the settings or overclocking your Pi, illustrated with a 2B model.

1. On the Pi's desktop, open your Pi's terminal.

2. Type in `cat /proc/ cpuinfo` then hit Enter. You then see your Pi's current settings – the processor normally runs at around 700 MHz.

Step 3: You can choose to overclock your Raspberry Pi.

3. You can choose to overclock the processor and/or the RAM.

4. Type in `vcgencmd get_config arm_freq` to check whether your Pi has any `arm_freq` settings already.

5. Type `sudo nano /boot/ config.txt`

6. Scroll down and find the line mentioning 'overclock'.

7. Remove the # to activate the overclock. Or type `arm_freq=800`

8. To overclock your RAM, go down one line and type `sdram_freq=300`

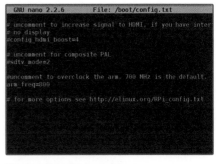

Step 7: Activate the overclock.

9. Hit Ctrl and X to exit. The Pi asks whether you want to save, so type Y for yes. It then asks whether you want to overwrite the original file, so type `enter` to do this.

10. For these changes to take effect, restart the Pi by typing `sudo shutdown -h now`

11. If you have an older version of the Pi and the changes haven't taken effect, go back into the Pi's Terminal and type `sudo sync`

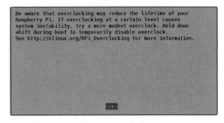

Step 12: Type in the relevant commands.

12. Then type `sudo sh -c "echo > /proc/sys/vm/drop_caches` then `enter`

13. Type `sudo cp/config.txt /boot config.txt.save` – the `config.txt` part should be the same as the file you saved your Pi settings under.

Step 15: Type the final commands, then restart the Pi.

14. Type the same command with `.1` at the end, so it becomes `sudo cp/config.txt /boot config.txt.save.1`

15. Type `sudo sync` then type `sync` and finish by restarting the Pi.

BREADBOARDING

A breadboard is a plastic board that enables you to test out simple circuits quickly and easily without soldering. The advantage of a breadboard is that you don't need to know how to solder, and you don't have to commit to the final connections before creating your desired circuit.

Hot Tip

LEDs are light emitting diodes. Electricity only passes through one way, so ensure it's the right way round. The longer leg goes to the positive side; the shorter leg goes to the negative.

BREADBOARD LAYOUT

The two inside sections are electronically connected (often labelled red) and the outer sections are generally used for power (marked with blue or black).

Sometimes power will only run halfway up the board, so connect the two sections with a wire to get power at the other end. It's advisable to keep the outer sections reserved for power to avoid confusion.

What Could You Use a Breadboard For?

There are lots of projects where you can use your Pi and a breadboard. It's a great tool for beginners and here are some projects that might be worth trying out:

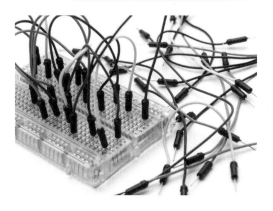

- ○ Morse code on LEDs
- ○ LED traffic lights
- ○ Buttons and switches

What Do You Need for a Basic Breadboard Project?

For a basic Pi breadboard project, you need the following items, which can be purchased from Amazon, eBay, BitsBox.co.uk or CoolComponents.co.uk:

- A Raspberry Pi
- Breadboard
- Two wires
- LED
- 220, 270 or 330 Ω (ohm) resistor

Build a Simple Circuit with Your Raspberry Pi

1. Connect a wire from the Pi's GPIO-17 to the breadboard.
2. Then plug in the LED next to your first wire on the breadboard.
3. Connect the 270 Ω resistor to the breadboard's ground (GND).
4. Connect a final wire from the breadboard to the Pi's GND.
5. Download and install WiringPi from wiringpi.com, which will help your Pi understand commands to switch on your LED.
6. Type in the following commands to your Pi's terminal.
7. `gpio mode 0 out`
8. `gpio write 0 1`
9. `gpio write 0 0`
10. Your LED should come on and go off again.

Resources for Breadboard Projects

- rpi.tnet.com
- www.cl.cam.ac.uk/projects/raspberrypi/tutorials/robot/breadboard/
- www.youtube.com/element14

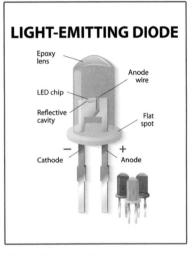

Above: LED stands for 'light emitting diode'.

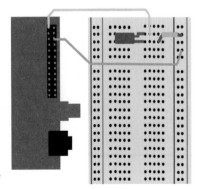

Above: This is the final circuit.

WHAT IS ARDUINO?

Arduino is an open source piece of hardware hailing from a company called SmartProjects in Italy. It's designed to be easy to use and can be deployed to create digital services and interactive objects. Its uses range from activating an LED to switching on a motor or even reacting to a message from Twitter.

Because Arduino is open source, its huge community has developed it to work on even more complicated projects, from doors that only open with a secret knock to programs that enable you to draw using eye movements.

BENEFITS OF ARDUINO

Overall, Arduino is good for fast, simple and easy projects, because it doesn't require as much code as the Raspberry Pi, but it won't be the right choice for more advanced projects. Arduino's software works with Windows, Macintosh OSX and Linux, whereas most microcontrollers are limited to Windows.

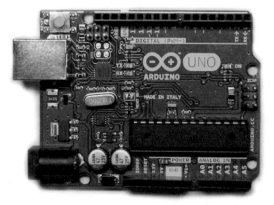

Above: The Arduino Uno R3 microcontroller.

Arduino vs Pi

The Raspberry Pi is a fully functioning computer, while Arduino is a microcontroller, which is a single component of a computer. The Pi is considerably faster and has 128,000 times more RAM. Arduino is better for simple hardware projects, such as getting an LED to light up.

The same task with a Pi would require an operating system and code libraries; whereas Arduino would take eight lines of code, because it isn't designed to use an OS. Arduino can only handle one task at a time, but the Pi can manage multiple projects. For this reason, Arduino is often recommended to beginners.

	Arduino Uno	Raspberry Pi 3 B
Price	£20 ($30)	£32 ($41)
Size	7.6 x 1.9 x 6.4 cm (3 x ¾ x 2½ in)	8.6 x 5.4 x 1.7 cm (3¼ x 2 x ¾ in)
Memory	0.002 MB	1 GB
Clock Speed	16 MHz	1.2 GHz
On Board Network	None	Ethernet, 802.11 bgn Wireless LAN
Multitasking	No	Yes
Input Voltage	7 to 12 V	+5.1 V micro USB supply
Flash	32 KB	Micro SD port up to 32GB
USB	One, input only	Four
Operating System	None	Linux, Windows
Integrated Development Environment	Arduino	Scratch, IDLE, anything with Linux support

Above: The specs of the Raspberry Pi compared to those of Arduino.

Using Arduino with the Pi

You can use the two devices in tandem. For instance, Arduino can drive a motor or LED, while the Raspberry Pi sends out the commands – blink, switch on, and so on – while simultaneously fulfilling your other needs and commands.

Above: The ATmega328P Arduino Board.

SOLDERING

Soldering is the process of melting metal in order to join two or more metal components together. It might be necessary when connecting add-on boards, or other components that don't come pre-assembled, to your Raspberry Pi.

EQUIPMENT

In order to start soldering, you need the following:

- Soldering iron
- Soldering iron stand
- Solder
- Cardboard to protect the surface you're working on
- A damp sponge to wipe your soldering iron with

Above: A soldering iron in its stand.

Soldering Project Ideas

- Portable camera
- LED Christmas tree
- Raspberry Pi robots
- Breakout boards

Make an LED Christmas Tree

You need the previously listed equipment, along with some wire cutters and a GPIO Christmas tree kit, which is available from DawnRobotics. co.uk.

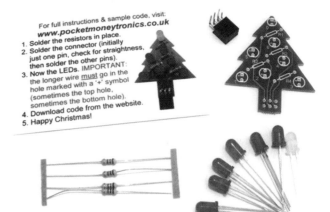

For full instructions & sample code, visit:
www.pocketmoneytronics.co.uk
1. Solder the resistors in place.
2. Solder the connector (initially just one pin, check for straightness, then solder the other pins).
3. Now the LEDs. IMPORTANT: the longer wire <u>must</u> go in the hole marked with a '+' symbol (sometimes the top hole, sometimes the bottom hole).
4. Download code from the website.
5. Happy Christmas!

Above: LED GPIO Xmas tree kit by PocketMoneyElectronics.

1. Take a resistor, bend it into an arch shape, then slot it through the corresponding hole marked on the back of the Christmas tree GPIO.

2. Flip over the GPIO. You can tape it to your worktop to make soldering easier.

3. Put your heated soldering iron into the joint first, then feed in the solder. Once the solder is in place, remove it and then remove the soldering iron.

4. Now snip the resistor's lead with your wire cutters.

5. Do the same process for the other side of the resistor, then continue soldering and clipping the other four resistors.

6. Put the connector on the front of the Christmas tree, making sure it's aligned so that it's straight.

7. Solder one of the corner pins, make sure the connector is straight, then solder the other pins.

8. Place each LED into its marked area. The long wire should go in the + hole and the short wire should go into the unmarked hole.

Hot Tip

It's recommended to start by practising on old circuit boards, but if you do go wrong, you can purchase solder-removing wick or a vacuum tube to fix mistakes.

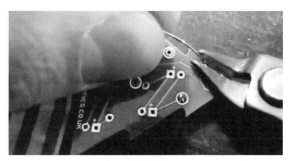

Step 4: Snip the resistor's lead.

.**Step 6**: Put the connector on the front of the tree.

9. Bear in mind that the slot for LED 2 is the other way around, so ensure that you place the LED in the correct way.

10. It might be worth taping down the LED, so that it doesn't fall out when you turn it over for soldering.

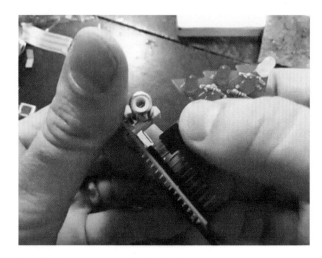

11. Continue soldering the LEDs and clipping their wires.

12. Connect your Christmas tree to the row of pins on your Raspberry Pi. Place it on the end of the row, as far as possible from the corner.

Step 12: Connect your tree to the Raspberry Pi.

13. On your Pi, create and browse to a folder called `xmas`.

14. Type in `mkdir xmas, cd xmas`

15. Download this file: www.pocketmoneytronics.co.uk/downloads/xmas.zip

16. Remove the zip file to the current directory with `unzip xmas.zip`

17. To see a list of example scripts, type `ls`

18. Run a script by typing `sudo python example_5.py`

19. Your LEDs should now be flashing. Merry Christmas!

Use a Mini GPIO Board

This board is available from
PocketMoneyElectronics.co.uk.

1. Solder your resistors into place. Remember to put your heated soldering iron into the joint first, then feed in the solder. Then remove the solder, followed by the iron.

2. Solder the push button into the top slot, next to 'B+' on the printed circuit board (PCB).

3. Solder the remaining three slots with the LEDs – the red one should go next to the push button, then the yellow, then the green.

4. Ensure that you insert the longer leg of the LED into the hole marked with a '+'.

5. Now solder the GPIO connector into place; ensure it goes on the opposite side of the PCB from all the other parts.

6. Now mount the board on to your Raspberry Pi.

7. Now you need to activate the LEDs. First, create a file called basic.py

8. Enter the code from the screenshot, then run the code by typing sudo python basic.py

Step 3: Solder in the LEDs.

```
1   # flash LEDs in sequence on the CLAS board for B+
2
3   import RPi.GPIO as GPIO
4   import time
5
6   GPIO.setmode(GPIO.BCM)
7
8   # GPIO allocations
9   button = 22
10  red = 10
11  yellow = 11
12  green = 5
13
14  # set the LED pins as outputs...
15  GPIO.setup(red, GPIO.OUT)
16  GPIO.setup(yellow, GPIO.OUT)
17  GPIO.setup(green, GPIO.OUT)
18  # ...and the button as an input (note: the button
19  # requires use of the Pi's internal pull-up resistor)
20  GPIO.setup(button, GPIO.IN, pull_up_down = GPIO.PUD_UP)
21
22  def check_button_and_pause():
23    if (GPIO.input(button)):
24      # button NOT pressed
25      time.sleep(1)
26    else:
27      # button IS pressed
28      time.sleep(0.1)
29
30  for i in range(10):
31    GPIO.output(red, 1) # red on
32    check_button_and_pause()
33    GPIO.output(red, 0) # red off
34
35    GPIO.output(yellow, 1) # yellow on
36    check_button_and_pause()
37    GPIO.output(yellow, 0) # yellow off
38
39    GPIO.output(green, 1) # green on
40    check_button_and_pause()
41    GPIO.output(green, 0) # green off
42
43  GPIO.cleanup()
```

Step 8: Enter this code.

RASPBERRY PI PERIPHERALS

There are plenty of weird and wonderful attachments for your Raspberry Pi. Some are more complex than others, but there are lots of affordable options to experiment with. Here are five peripherals that can work as a good starting point and allow you to move on to more advanced projects in the future.

TOUCHSCREEN

A touchscreen enables you to quickly access your Raspberry Pi's interface, to make small changes and activate different commands. You can also use it to play video and display images.

How Much are They?

There are plenty of options at different price points. The ones at the lower end of the scale have a lower resolution screen, but only cost around £20 ($35), while larger 10-inch screens cost about £70 ($110).

Above: The PiTFT touchscreen.

Recommendations and Specs

To start with, we recommend the 2.8-inch PiTFT TFT+Touchscreen. The display has a 16-bit colour screen, which comes with a stylus. It can be an interface or video player, or display messages. The touchscreen works with Pi Model A or B, as well as Pi 2 or Pi 1 Model B+.

Above: Fitting the PiTFT touchscreen.

The great thing about this screen is that you can plug it straight into your Pi's GPIOs and get started. The only other thing required is to download and install the kernel OS for the screen.

Touchscreen Projects

- **Web browser:** You can set up the touchscreen in the same way you would a smartphone or tablet to browse the internet.

- **Media player:** A touchscreen is also sufficient for watching movies and TV shows – although you might want a higher-resolution screen for this.

- **Make a smartphone:** If you do decide to invest in a better quality screen, you can essentially make your own tablet or smartphone (*see* more on this in Chapter 4, page 110).

- **Gaming:** This kind of screen is ideal for mobile gaming.

- **Messages and slogans:** The simple screen can flash messages, too, so you could create signs or a T-shirt with an animated message, to advertise wherever you roam.

CAMERA

There's a whole host of ways you can incorporate cameras into your Raspberry Pi set-up, and plenty of projects to apply them to.

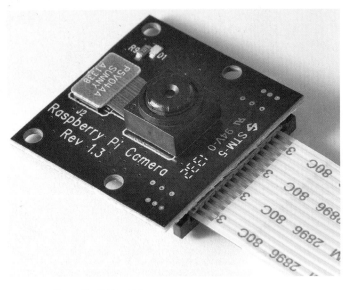

Above: The NoIR camera.

How Much are They?

Pi cameras range between £20 and £30 (about $30 to $45) in price, depending on what functionality you want.

Set-up and Installation

All camera peripherals connect to your Pi via the two small sockets on the board's upper surface. They all come fully assembled and ready to plug into your Pi, and they can be set up with a few commands using your existing Raspbian image.

What's Available?

- **Camera Board**: This standard five-megapixel Camera Board can capture 2,592 x 1,944 pixel images and up to 1080p video.

- **NoIR Camera**: This camera can capture infrared images and video, so it's ideal for working outdoors, although you need infrared lighting.

- **Spy Camera**: This tiny snapper is the size of a five pence piece and comes with a longer cable – 289 mm or 11.4 in – so you can station the Pi further away.

Camera Projects

- **Webcam**: The standard Camera Board can be used as a webcam for video chats and capturing your own pictures for social media or blogging.

- **Security camera**: The size and cost of the Pi and cameras make them ideal for setting up your own security cameras.

- **Time-lapse photography**: You can use the Pi to capture time-lapse images to document a plant growing or building work over a long period.

Above: The Camera Board.

- **Nature photography**: The NoIR camera is great for recording wildlife because it can capture images in the dark, although it needs infrared lighting.

- **Hyperspectral imaging**: The camera collects data across the electromagnetic spectrum. It can be used to identify materials for medical, geological and various other scientific pursuits.

- **Spy camera**: This affords plenty of opportunities to nestle a camera where it won't be seen, perhaps as a baby monitor hidden in a teddy or a car dashboard camera.

Above: The NoIR camera is ideal for capturing wildlife in the dark.

RGB MATRIX HATS

If you want your Raspberry Pi to do amazing things on the outside, just like it does on the inside, the colourful LED displays of the RGB Matrix HATs might be worth considering.

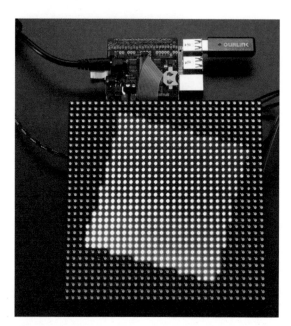

Above: The RGB Matrix.

How Much are They?

Matrix HATs are available for around £16 ($25) for the 16 x 32 RGB LED variety. They can cost around £50 ($80) for the 32 x 32 versions, and the largest versions, which can also bend, range between £64 and £200 (about $100 and $300).

Set-up and Installation

The RGB LED Matrix peripherals display up to 32 x 128 pixels. The hardware enables you to string a series of Matrices together, but one Pi can handle only four of them in total. A separate 5 V power supply is needed, because the Pi can't power the Matrix on its own.

The Matrix might require an additional HAT attachment. These require some soldering, which can be done relatively quickly. It's worth noting that these HATs only work with the Raspberry Pi Model A+ or B+.

Hot Tip

Additional hardware for your Raspberry Pi is sometimes referred to as a HAT – this stands for Hardware on Top. HATs can add extra connections and functionality to your Pi.

Above: The NeoPixel RGB LED Matrix.

Matrix Pi Projects

- **Video wall:** By combining multiple Pis and Matrix HATs, you can create a video wall. This can display decorative designs or even scroll through messages.

- **Digital clock:** You can make your own retro time and date display. The RGB Matrix attachments come with a real-time clock, so they keep track of the time, even if the Pi is turned off.

- **RSS feeds:** Matrix HATs can be set up to display RSS feeds from your favourite websites or social media, and you can program them to filter through the different stories at timed intervals.

- **Artwork:** You can command Matrix HATs to put on dazzling 16-bit light displays of your own design, or pre-programmed ones.

- **Signs:** It's possible to make your own animated signs for stands or small shops at events.

GESTURE SENSORS

Gesture sensors enable you to control your Raspberry Pi using simple hand movements. The sensor uses electrodes to pick up your gestures from up to 5 cm away.

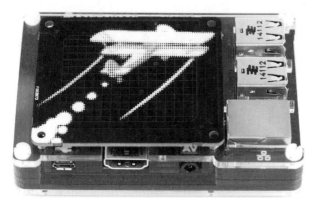

Above: The Skywriter HAT from Amazon.co.uk.

These sensors can read left, right, up and down swiping gestures. They also register double-taps and multi-touch interactions. They can be used to control output or as an input method for controlling programs.

How Much are They?

The Pimoroni Skywriter HAT from Adafruit.com costs around £13 ($21) and comes fully assembled.

Set-up and Installation

The sensor is simple to set up and easily plugs into the top of the Raspberry Pi. It's compatible with Python's API, requires a few lines of code to activate and the kit works with a Raspberry Pi 1, 2, A+, B+ and Pi 3.

Above: The Skywriter HAT from Amazon.co.uk.

Gesture Sensor Projects

- **Speaker volume**: The gesture sensor can be used to alter volume on your speaker system and even control the levels and pitch of a noise, in a similar way to an orchestra conductor.

- **Control unit**: The sensor can also be used with other kit to control operations. For instance, you can have an LED screen displaying arrow directions corresponding to your hand movements.

- **Make animations**: Add a Raspberry Pi camera and use the gesture sensor to track your movements and replicate them on a computer screen using animation.

- **Control programs wirelessly**: This technique enables you to spin a 3D globe on screen, or manipulate Google Earth.

- **Airborne artwork**: The gesture sensor can control art tools, enabling you to create images and designs in the air.

- **Air guitar**: The gesture sensor HAT can also be used to trigger audio clips to create a literal air guitar.

Hot Tip

The gesture sensor can be used up to 5 cm away, so it can still function behind non-conductive materials, such as fabrics or acrylic.

CAPACITIVE TOUCH HAT

This HAT is touchable, allowing your Raspberry Pi to sense touch interactions from up to 12 sensors. This works by registering when a person – or animal – has come into contact with one of the sensor electrodes. This is the same sort of technology that's used for touchscreen phones, tablets and computers.

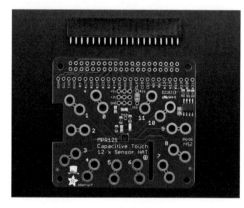

Above: The Adafruit Capacitive Touch HAT.

How Much are They?

We recommend the Adafruit Capacitive Touch HAT for Raspberry Pi mini kit, which retails at just under £10 ($15).

Set-up and Installation

The Capacitive Touch HAT has 12 holes with electrodes, which can be gripped using alligator clip cables. The kit requires light soldering to attach the socket headers to the HAT circuit board.

The Capacitive Touch HAT works well with the Raspberry Pi Model A+, B+ or Pi 2. It also works with the Raspberry Pi Model A or B, though they require some extra soldering.

Capacitive Touch HAT Projects

- **Fruit drum kit:** Connect to the HAT's sensor holes via an alligator clip, then attach the clip to your chosen sensor. Metal, fruit or anything that contains water can be used, including a jug of water.

- **Link buttons:** You can create touchable links, which trigger websites to open.

○ **Touch-launched video**: The Touch HAT can be used to launch specific video clips or display certain images.

○ **Light switch**: This kit can also be used to activate lights, from LEDs to more elaborate light set-ups.

○ **Open doors**: You can trigger a door to unlock by setting up a specific secret knock as an input method.

○ **Presentations**: This could help with a presentation, for example, different touch sensors could play information about various areas of a map.

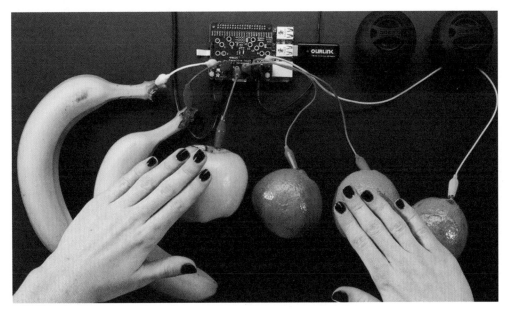

Above: Play the drums on fruit.

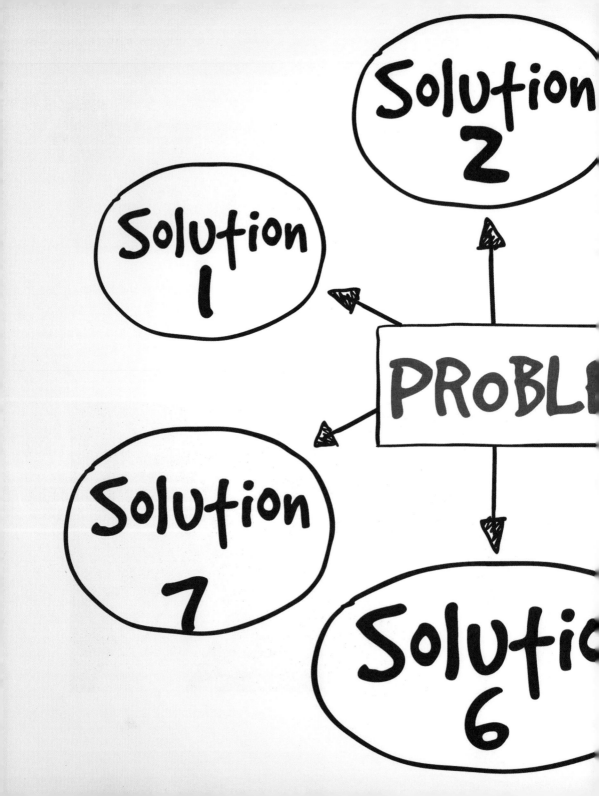

TROUBLESHOOTING

FOR WHEN THINGS GO WRONG

The Pi is a reliable little device, but at times – inevitably – you will run into problems. Use this chapter to help fix common issues (the Raspberry Pi forums are a good choice for more unusual errors). Most problems with the Pi are relatively straightforward to fix, so rather than return the device as faulty, roll up your sleeves and have a go yourself.

FIRST STEPS FOR ANY PROBLEM

Check Your Power Supply

Ensure your power is from a reliable, branded 5 V supply. Many unbranded power supplies do not provide the voltage they claim to, which leads to insufficient power for your Pi.

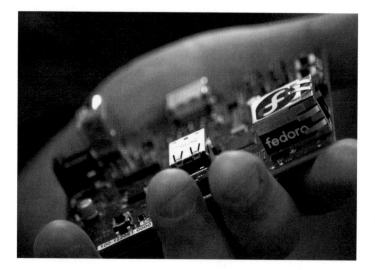

Above: Don't return a faulty Pi until you've tried to fix the problem on your own.

Stay Up to Date

Many 'faulty' Pis are in fact using SD cards with out-of-date images bought from a third party. Beware of buying pre-flashed SD cards from Amazon, eBay or other unofficial outlets. To fix, format your SD card using one of many available tools (tinyurl.com/SDcardformat) and install the Raspbian operating system using NOOBS (instructions: tinyurl.com/NOOBSinstall).

COMMON PROBLEMS

Over the following pages we'll take a look at some of the common problems you might come across and guide you through how to solve them.

WI-FI ISSUES

Here's a step-by-step guide for troubleshooting common Wi-Fi problems. This assumes you are using the Pi 3 or Pi Zero W with onboard Wi-Fi.

Above: The inbuilt Wi-Fi antenna on the Pi 3 means no more USB dongles.

1. Check your router is working correctly, try restarting it if not.

2. If this fails, plug in an Ethernet cable, test that you have wired internet, then open Terminal. Type:

```
sudo ifdown wlan0 sudo ifup wlan0
```

3. If that fails, try updating your software packages with the following command:

```
sudo apt-get update sudo apt-get upgrade sudo apt-get dist-
upgrade sudo rpi-update sudo reboot.
```

Wait for reboot, then type:

```
sudo branch=next rpi-update sudo reboot
```

4. A handy tool for managing Wireless and Wired connections is wicd. You can get this GUI program by executing the following: `sudo apt-get install wicd`

TROUBLESHOOTING USING PI LEDS

The Raspberry Pi has five built-in LEDs – near its USB connector – that can help you identify problems with the device. They are especially useful with power or start-up problems.

○ **Green LED**: Flashes when the SD card is active.

○ **Red LED**: Lights up when the Pi is receiving power.

○ **FDX orange LED**: On when there is full duplex.

○ **LNK orange LED**: On when Ethernet is connected.

○ **100 orange LED**: On when the connection is 100 Mbps; off when it is 10 Mbps.

This section deals with interpreting changes in LED patterns.

Above: The red PWR LED, near the USB connector, is useful for diagnosing power problems.

Red LED Flashes

This indicates a power supply issue. On Models A and B, it means your 5 V power supply is failing, and you should try to replace your supply. On other models, the LED flashes or turns off when the voltage falls below 4.63 V. Check all your connections, cables and power supply.

Red LED On, Faint Steady Green LED, No Display

Your Pi has not executed a boot code. Complete each of these steps until the problem is fixed.

1. The Raspberry Pi may not be able to find a valid SD card image. Turn the Pi over and ensure that the SD card is properly inserted. Use a PC or Mac to browse the card, looking for bootcode.bin, fixup.dat and start.elf.

2. Ensure you have admin rights for whatever software you used to write the image to the SD card.

3. Your image may be corrupted. Search for a checksum utility, download it and use it on the image.

4. Your SD card may not work with the Pi. Search online for a list of compatible SD cards and – if necessary – replace the card.

5. One of your USB devices or cables may be interfering with your Pi, so unplug them and plug them in one by one, testing until you have found the culprit.

6. The issue can be caused by an improperly seated card, due to solder residue under the contact. Insert a pin under each contact and pull upwards lightly, until one end of the SD contact comes away. Blow into each cavity to clear residue, and push the contact back into place.

7. Check your SD card for cracks. These can cause your SD to become improperly seated within your Pi. Hold the SD card in place manually and boot up to confirm the problem.

8. Your bootcode.bin file may be bugged – download the version at tinyurl.com/bootcodebin.

9. Cold temperatures can cause fractures in the board. Heat the Pi with a hairdryer for a few seconds and reconnect the power.

10. *See* 'Troubleshooting Power Problems', pages 250–51.

Step 9: Try heating the Pi with a hairdryer.

Green LED Blinking in Specific Pattern

- **One flash**: It could indicate a problem with a Micron Raspberry Pi. Download the latest software on to your Pi, and ensure you're using at least a 4 GB SD card.

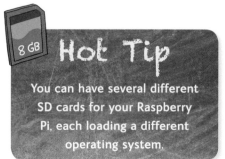

- **Two flashes**: The Pi cannot read your SD card. Format your card, by searching for an SD card formatter online, and install Raspbian following the instructions on the Foundation's website (tinyurl.com/PiInstaller).

OTHER START-UP ISSUES

Coloured Splash Screen

If the splash screen hangs on start-up, it could mean the kernel.img file is failing to boot – try replacing it with another.

Try replacing the file by changing the config.txt file on the SD card. Use a PC to load the file, and add `boot_delay=1`.

Alternatively, you can use another Pi to add the text by running `sudo nano /boot/config.txt`.

Above: If your splash screen hangs, you may have a problem with your kernel.img file.

See 'Troubleshooting Power Problems' on pages 250–51.

Pi Shuts Down/Restarts After Booting

This is caused by too low a voltage from the power supply. *See* 'Troubleshooting Power Problems' on pages 250–51.

Errors After Running Startx

Ensure you have free space on your SD card, because it may be full.

Kernel Panic

Text appears on the screen and stays, along with a 'Kernel panic' message. This is often caused by USB devices attached to the Pi. Remove all USB devices, and re-attach them one by one.

Pi Boots Sporadically

Some users experience normal boots occasionally but at other times their device fails to start.

The issue remains largely unresolved, and can be caused by low voltage or a faulty SD card. Ensure you use an SD card from a reliable manufacturer and buy from a reliable source.

You could try cleaning the SD card contacts on the Pi, because the issue can be caused by an improperly seated card, due to solder residue under the contact. *See* page 241, step 6.

Above: Many users report problems trying to boot their Raspberry Pi.

SOUND

Sound Does Not Work with HDMI Monitor

Some monitors select DVI mode automatically. To force HDMI mode, edit your config.txt file by running the command `sudo nano /boot/config.txt` and add the following three lines to the file:

```
hdmi_drive=2
hdmi_force_hotplug=1
hdmi_force_edid_audio=1
```

No Sound in Some/All Applications

1. Run the command `alsamixer` and check that the Pi is not muted and the volume is up.

> **Hot Tip**
>
> The Pi plays only WAV sound files by default – download an MP3 player for MP3 files.

2. Raspbian may disable sound by default. In the command line, type:

```
sudo apt-get update
sudo apt-get upgrade
sudo apt-get install alsa-utils
```

3. Type `aplay /usr/share/sounds/alsa/Front_Center.wav` into the command line.

4. Force sound to a specific output by typing the command `amixer cset numid=3 <n>`, where n is 0 for automatic, 1 for headphones and 2 for HDMI.

DISPLAY

Large Borders on HD Monitors

Pi graphics may not fill your monitor by default because of underscan. The solution may be as easy as disabling overscan on your monitor/TV's settings directly. Note: it may go by a different name, such as 'just scan', 'screen fit' or 'HD size'.

If this does not work, you need to edit your config.txt file.

Above: If the graphics don't fill the monitor, it may be due to underscan.

1. Type `sudo nano /boot/config.txt` in the command line to open the file.

2. Add `disable_overscan=1` to the file.

3. Add a # to all other overscan lines in the file, for example: `#overscan_left=10`. Save and reboot. This should fix the problem on most displays.

4. If this does not work, adjust the overscan parameters in the config.txt file to centre the picture. These are, where `n` is a number:
   `overscan_left=n`
   `overscan_right=n`
   `overscan_top=n`
   `overscan_bottom=n`
   Adjust `n` to centre the picture. A more negative value reduces black borders.

Above: Display interference can be caused by using HDMI cables that are too long.

Writing Goes Off the Side of the Display

The opposite of the problem on the previous page: your Pi's graphics may be larger than your screen because of overscan. Follow the instructions in step 4 on the previous page, but make the n values larger.

Display Interference

If you see fuzziness or grouped white spots on your display, it may be caused by a loss of video signal in long cables, or loss of signal because of adapters. You can fix this by editing your config.txt file.

1. Type `sudo nano /boot/config.txt` in the command line.

2. Add `config_hdmi_boost=n` to the file, with n varying from 1 to 7, depending on the length of the cable: 1 for very short, 7 for very long. You can have a value above 7, but it may cause damage to your monitor. Use high values to negate signal loss in adapters, too.

3. *See* 'Troubleshooting Power Problems' on pages 250–51.

No HDMI Output at All

There are lots of options for solving this problem:

1. Try connecting the HDMI without a case on your Pi, because it can stop a proper connection.

Above: If you can't get any output from your HDMI, take the case off your Pi and try connecting the cable again.

2. Add `config_hdmi_boost=n` to config.txt – *see* step 1 of 'Display Interference'. Try an n value of 4 first, and gradually increase to a maximum of 7.

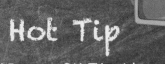

3. Try adding `hdmi_force_hotplug=1` to your config file.

4. *See* 'Troubleshooting Power Problems', pages 250–51.

No Display Using Composite

Again, there are many potential fixes for no display when using the composite output. First check your cables to ensure they are properly inserted. Then try the following:

1. Disconnect any HDMI cables from the Pi, because they cause the Pi to default to HDMI output.

2. Your Pi may be forcing an HDMI output. Inspect the config.txt file for `hdmi_force_hotplug=1` and comment it by adding a # at the start.

3. Ensure you have the right mode on your monitor – normally AV.

KEYBOARD AND MOUSE PROBLEMS

Pi Does Not Respond to Key Presses

This is most commonly caused by issues with the power supply. Ensure you use a reliable, branded power supply and USB lead (not a mobile phone lead). Try disconnecting every other USB device and see whether the keyboard works. If it doesn't, check your keyboard for a label showing voltage and mA requirements – these should be a maximum of 5 V and 100 mA, otherwise older Pis cannot support them.

> ### Hot Tip
> Linux distributions do not show that you have entered any characters when typing your password. Try typing your username to verify your keyboard is working.

Keyboard Responds Erratically

Some users have reported Pis repeating or skipping their key presses. One potential fix is to adjust the USB bus speed. Access the cmdline.txt file, found in the /boot directory, and add `dwc_otg.speed=1` at the end of the text.

Sticky Keys

If you're encountering sticky keys when using the device – when separate key presses are identified as happening together – update the firmware on your SD card using `rpi-update`. To install under Raspbian, run `sudo apt-get install rpi-update` then run `sudo rpi-update` to update the firmware.

Hot Tip

Keyboards with backlights may consume too much power, so use one without.

Slow Keyboard Mapping

If you have remapped your keyboard, and face long delays at start-up during keyboard mapping, simply type `sudo setupcon` in the command line once.

Keyboard and Mouse Interfering with Wi-Fi

Plugging in a USB keyboard or mouse when a USB Wi-Fi device is connected can cause your Pi to fail. This could be a power problem, so make sure you're using a branded, 5 V power supply, or try a powered hub.

It may also be down to interference with the 2.4 GHz band used by both USB keyboards/mice and Wi-Fi sticks. To attempt a fix, change the channel on your wireless access point.

TROUBLESHOOTING POWER PROBLEMS

Power trouble can cause a plague of Pi problems. The first thing you'll want to do if you suspect a failure is to test the voltage, using a multimeter. If you have never used a multimeter before, *see* tinyurl.com/howtomultimeter. Use the test points TP1 and TP2 on the Pi circuit board to test the voltage.

Above: A multimeter is essential for troubleshooting power problems.

Set your multimeter to the range 20 V direct current, and test when the Pi is active. You should get a voltage reading between 4.75 and 5.25 V – anything outside indicates a problem.

- **Check your power supply:** Make sure it is labelled as at least 700 mA.

- **Your power supply may not be supplying enough voltage:** It might need replacing.

- **Detach USB devices and test again:** They may need too much power – the Pi can only handle up to 100 mA USB devices.

- **Test the polyfuse:** It could be blown – *see* the next page for how to test it.

Testing the Polyfuse

1. Remove anything plugged into your Pi, including the SD card.

2. Locate the TP2 test points on the top and bottom of your board.

3. Plug in your power supply.

4. Place one lead of the multimeter on the bottom TP2 point.

5. Place the other lead on the F3 fuse (labelled, next to the SD card slot). First try the side closest to the edge of the board. Then try the side next to the SD card slot.

6. If the difference between the two readings is more than 0.3 V, there is a problem with your fuse. A blown fuse fixes itself, but can take up to an hour. Test again later in the day. If the test consistently shows problems, your board probably came with a faulty fuse, so contact the supplier.

> **Hot Tip**
>
> A polyfuse is a fuse made from polymer, designed to heal itself when blown.

Above: The polyfuse is labelled F3, to the left of the SD card.

FURTHER READING

Cox, Tim, *Raspberry Pi Cookbook for Python Programmers*, Packt Publishing, 2014

Johnson, Sydney, *Raspberry Pi: A Beginner's Guide to the Raspberry Pi*, CreateSpace Independent Publishing Platform, 2014

McGrath, Mike, *Raspberry Pi in Easy Steps*, In Easy Steps Limited, 2013

McManus, Sean, *Raspberry Pi for Dummies*, John Wiley and Sons, 2014

Membrey, Peter and Hows, David, *Learn Raspberry Pi with Linux*, Apress, 2013

Monk, Simon, *Programming the Raspberry Pi: Getting Started with Python*, Tab Electronics, 2013

Monk, Simon, *Raspberry Pi Cookbook*, O'Reilly Media, 2014

Norris, Donald, *Raspberry Pi Projects for the Evil Genius*, Tab Electronics, 2013

Oates, Matthew, *Raspberry Pi for Beginners*, CreateSpace Independent Publishing Platform, 2015

Pappachen, James, *et al.*, *An Introductory Guide to Raspberry Pi*, CreateSpace Independent Publishing Platform, 2015

Richardson, Matt and Wallace, Shawn, *Getting Started with Raspberry Pi*, Maker Media, Inc., 2013

Robinson, Andrew and Cook, Mike, *Raspberry Pi Projects*, Wiley, 2013

Suehle, Ruth and Callaway, Tom, *Raspberry Pi Hacks: Tips and Tools for Making Things with the Inexpensive Linux Computer*, O'Reilly Media, 2014

Upton, Eben, *Raspberry Pi User Guide*, John Wiley and Sons, 2014

Upton, Eben, Upton, Liz and Girling, Gray, *Raspberry Pi Manual: a Practical Guide to the Revolutionary Small Computer*, J.H. Haynes & Co Ltd, 2013

Wentk, Richard, *Teach Yourself Visually Raspberry Pi*, Visual, 2014

WEBSITES

www.adafruit.com
A fantastic website full of information about the Raspberry Pi, tutorials and projects to have a go at, and a shop to buy the Pi itself as well as accessories and pieces of kit.

www.gadgets.ndtv.com
If in need of advice on which gadget best suits you, this website offers helpful reviews and news on everything tech related.

www.theguardian.com/technology/raspberry-pi
Visit this site for information and support that can be found in a variety of articles, such as how you can get the most out of your Raspberry Pi.

www.howtogeek.com
This is an excellent site to visit if you are in need of easy-to-read guides for anything tech related, with straightforward articles and live discussion.

www.huffingtonpost.co.uk/news/gadget-comparisons
If you are looking to expand your gadget collection but are unsure as to where to start, this site is great for offering reviews and handy comparisons.

www.informationweek.com
A great site that shares news and expert knowledge on all things technical, as well as connecting the IT business community together through reviews, videos and interesting articles.

www.itpro.co.uk
This website offers you the latest news from the IT community and also has reviews on a range of PC related topics and gadgets.

www.lifehacker.com
For those who may not be IT experts, this site is great for offering useful and straightforward beginner guides to a range of technical equipment, including how to get to grips with the Raspberry Pi.

www.neil-black.co.uk
If in need of Raspberry Pi advice, this tech focused blog is a great starting point for covering common problems or any related queries you may have.

www.pcadvisor.co.uk
Head to this website for technology reviews, helpful tutorials and any general IT support that you may need.

www.penguintutor.com/linux/raspberrypi
This website provides a basic introduction to the Raspberry Pi which is really ideal for any first time users.

www.pimylifeup.com
Interested in starting a project with the Raspberry Pi? This website will offer several potential ideas.

www.raspberrypi.org/blog/tag/kids
A helpful and friendly blog that will help children learn more about their Raspberry Pi as well as give them ideas for fun and innovative projects that they can get underway with.

www.raspberrypi.org/forums
A useful forum offering support and advice on everything Raspberry Pi related.

www.raspberrypi.org/help/quick-start-guide
This website offers general discussion, FAQs and regular blog updates on everything you need to know about the Raspberry Pi.

www.raspberrypihq.com
This website will offer you support and assistance with any Raspberry Pi problems you may have, as well as exciting potential project ideas that you can get to grips with.

www.recycleyourgadget.co.uk
If unsure about what to do with any old gadgets you may have tucked away, head to this site for ideas and advice on what to do with them.

www.techradar.com
A site that includes a helpful introduction of what the Raspberry Pi is, as well as other helpful tips and suggestions.

www.techspot.com
A great website that offers general information for any technical problems that you may have.

INDEX